The
Future
of
Christian
Faith
in
America

DAVID YOUNT

Augsburg Books
MINNEAPOLIS

Also by David Yount

GROWING IN FAITH
A Guide for the Reluctant Christian

BREAKING THROUGH GOD'S SILENCE
A Guide to Effective Prayer

SPIRITUAL SIMPLICITY
Simplify Your Life and Refresh Your Spirit

TEN THOUGHTS TO TAKE INTO ETERNITY
Living Wisely in Light of the Afterlife

BE STRONG AND COURAGEOUS
Letters to My Children about Being Christian

WHAT ARE WE TO DO?
Living the Sermon on the Mount

FAITH UNDER FIRE
Religion's role in the American Dream

For David Bowes

Friendship is a sheltering tree.

THE FUTURE OF CHRISTIAN FAITH IN AMERICA

Large-quantity purchases or custom editions of this book are available at a discount from the publisher. For more information, contact the sales department at Augsburg Fortress, Publishers, 1-800-328-4648, or write to: Sales Director, Augsburg Fortress, Publishers, P.O. Box 1209, Minneapolis, MN 55440-1209.

ISBN 0-8066-4946-1

Cover design by Ann Rezny
Book design by Michelle L. N. Cook

The paper used in this publication meets the minimum requirements of American National Standard for Information Sciences—Permanence of Paper for Printed Library Materials, ANSI Z329.48-1984. ⊚ ™

Manufactured in the U.S.A.

08 07 06 05 04   1 2 3 4 5 6 7 8 9 10

Contents

*"It is all too evident that the religiousness
characteristic of America today
is very often a religiousness without religion,
a religiousness without almost any kind
of context or none, a way of sociability,
of 'belonging' rather than a way
of reorienting life to God . . .
a religiousness without serious commitment,
without real conviction,
without genuine existential decision."*

—Will Herberg, *Protestant, Catholic, Jew* (1960)

Chapter 1

One
Nation
under
God

"*We have become the kind of society that civilized countries used to send missionaries to.*"
—William J. Bennett[1]

THE CELEBRATED JEWISH SOCIOLOGIST WILL HERBERG MADE a classic survey of religion in America in the 1950s[2] when, to all appearances, the nation was celebrating its third historic Great Awakening to faith. In the wake of World War II, church attendance and church construction were at an all-time high. Four of every five Americans belonged to a church or synagogue, and half actually joined with their coreligionists in worship every week. Ten million copies of the Bible were distributed every year, a record. [3]

America's first Great Awakening occurred between 1730 and 1760 and was marked by a tidal wave of revivalism. Its sequel took place in the first thirty years of the nineteenth century, spurred by circuit riders taking the gospel to the American frontier.

Herberg concluded that, despite the renewed interest in religious faith in the mid-twentieth century, it was no Great Awakening. He found the faith of Americans, although widespread and sincerely held, to be typically shallow, sentimental, passive, self-serving, and uninformed. In the 1950s, although four of every five adults acknowledged the Bible as the "revealed word of God," a majority of Americans could not recall the name of even one of the four Gospels. [4]

President Eisenhower, launching the American Legion's "Back to God" movement in 1955, summoned religious faith to support patriotism, proclaiming that "recognition of the Supreme Being is the first, the most basic, expression of Americanism." [5] But the president was indifferent as to the content and object of faith as long as all citizens believed. Lamentably, most Americans half a century ago merely had faith in faith—the positive and comforting attitude of *believing*—not much more.

Herberg concluded that "the new religiosity pervading America seems to be very largely the religious validation of the social patterns and cultural values associated with the American Way of Life," serving as "a spiritual reinforcement of national self-righteousness and a spiritual authentication of national self-will." [6] Faith made people feel good about themselves.

In the intervening half-century, religious faith has become, if anything, shallower than it was in the 1950s, and the actual practice of faith has plummeted. Today the fraction of the population that spends any time on religion is only half of what it was in Herberg's time. By the 1990s the percentage of Americans who claimed to have "no religion" had increased more than five-fold.[7]

Effects of the Fallout

The fallout from faith has been felt beyond church doors, because traditionally half of all personal charity and half of all volunteering in America are church-related. Whereas four out of five church members give to charity, only three of five nonmembers do. Three-fifths of church members volunteer to serve those in need, but only one-third of nonmembers do.[8] Declining churchgoing translates into less generosity and less commitment to the needs of others.

Virtually all Americans, when asked, continue to express a belief in God, and three-fourths believe in immortality. But this faith is notional. As historian Martin Marty warns, "Unless religious impulses find a home in more than the individual heart and soul, they will have few long-lasting public consequences."[9]

In recent years sociologists began comparing what Americans say about their religious observance with actual counts of worshipers in the pews. Researchers concluded that the over-reporting of church attendance runs as high as 50 percent.[10]

As young adults, the Baby Boomers born after World War II were substantially more likely to be disaffected with religion than their parents at the same age. Fully two-thirds of Boomers raised in a religious tradition dropped out in early adulthood, and only half returned after settling into marriage and becoming responsible for families.[11] As sociologists Wade Clark Roof and William McKinney observe:

> Large numbers of young, well-educated, middleclass youth . . . "dropped out" of organized religion altogether in favor of highly individualized religious psychology without the benefits of strong supportive attachments to believing communities. A major impetus in this direction in the post-1960s was the thrust toward greater personal fulfillment and quest for the ideal self. . . . In this climate of excessive individualism, religion tends to become "privatized," or more anchored in personal realms.[12]

The Boomers' successors, the so-called Generation X, have only accelerated the departure from faith and observance. By century's end nearly one-fifth of college freshmen expressed no religious preference. Even in the early 1990s fewer than one in three high school students were worshiping regularly.[13]

The decline in faith and practice affects Protestants, Catholics, and Jews alike. As Harvard sociologist Robert D. Putnam notes, "More and more Catholics are becoming nominal church members, while a large and steadily growing number of Protestants and Jews are abandoning their religion altogether."[14]

A Disconnected Nation

In the wake of the tragedies of September 11, 2001, the president's wife appeared at the National Press Club to reassure the nation, but acknowledged the "self-indulgence" of Americans and reflected that "we're a different country than we were . . . sadder and less innocent."[15] Initially after September 11, many Americans returned to church for comfort and solidarity, but the fervor of faith was only temporary. The surge in patriotism clearly trumped any increase in religious observance.

It is no coincidence that over the past quarter-century the nation became disconnected at the same time religious faith and observance were in free fall. Political, civic, and social participation waned along with religious observance. The decline of community connection affects all generations from youth to the elderly. As a people, we are increasingly detached from family, friends, neighbors, and social structures, threatening our civic and personal health—not to mention our spiritual well-being.

As faith has declined, we are no longer the nation of belongers that Alexis de Tocqueville so admired in the nineteenth century. As we have separated from our neighbors, we have become disenchanted with our fellow man. A half-century ago a majority of Americans believed people in general lived honest and moral lives. Today only one-fourth of us claim to trust one another.[16]

The loosening of social bonds has already resulted in lower educational performance, more teen pregnancy and child suicide, low birth rate, increased prenatal mortality and crime rate, and declining health. With half of all marriages ending in divorce, we have severed the primary bond between man and woman, with devastating consequences for them and their children. The fashion for faith in oneself has degenerated into self-interest and self-indulgence, and left too many Americans alone and adrift. We have become a nation of unsocial, uninvolved stay-at-homes, and we are smothering in our cocoons.

The more we retreat from faith, the less generous we are with others. At century's end, despite a booming economy, Americans gave less to charity than at any time since the war years of the 1940s. Relative to what we spend on recreation, we contribute only half as much to needy causes as we did in the 1960s.[17] Americans not only concern themselves less with others, but are quicker to mistrust them and take offense. The back covers of telephone directories across the nation advertise lawyers who urge us to sue for damages.

A Faith Infected with Secularism

Even at the high watermark of faith in the mid-twentieth century, Herberg lamented that "the religion which actually prevails among Americans today has lost much of its authentic Christian or Jewish content. . . . Americans think, feel, and act in terms quite obviously secularist at the very time that they exhibit every sign of a widespread religious revival."[18]

Today religious publishing is still a vital industry, but most titles are inspirational rather than educational, appealing to sentiment rather than the mind. Visit any large bookstore and you will find New Age spirituality crowding out religious titles. As we shall see, New Age competes with religious faith and practice by celebrating the self, not the creator. Although New Age is actually inimical to religion, many Americans hold syncretic faiths, mixing traditional symbols with New Age optimism and self-indulgence. A majority of Americans not only believes that God helps those who help themselves, but holds erroneously that that prescription comes from Scripture.

In the early twenty-first century American faith is not only shallow and uninformed, but unauthentic. Christianity, Judaism, and Islam share the revelation that humankind is responsible to its creator, whereas popular faith is comfortable only with a creator who indulges his creatures. Popular piety likes to characterize itself as a lifelong "search" for self-sufficiency. The very tentativeness of "seeking" ensures lack of religious commitment and forgives faith's fuzziness. The common quest for meaning is typically no longer a search for God but for the self.

Whereas, as Herberg noted,

> The living God of Jewish-Christian faith is to be found not through self-sufficient "searching," but through "meeting" Him as He discloses Himself in the divine-human encounter of which Scripture and the traditions of the believing community are the witness. He is a God Who goes forth to "visit" man in the midst of life, and discloses Himself in the encounter.

He concludes:

> The God of the Bible makes his unconditional demand upon men, calls them to total love and obedience, and therewith also judges them in their self-interest and

self-aggrandizing pretensions. In Jewish-Christian faith, the word of redeeming grace comes only after the word of judgment has shattered all human claims to security and self-sufficiency.[19]

The Consequences of Faith

Herberg's demanding faith clearly does not reflect the mile-wide, inch-deep religion prevalent in America today. A 1993 poll revealed that 30 percent of Americans live only with secular values, even when they claim religious faith.

George Gallup Jr. refers to us as a "nation of biblical illiterates." Only four in ten Americans know that Jesus delivered the Sermon on the Mount. Only three in ten teenagers know why Easter is celebrated. Only three persons in ten look to Scripture for truth; two-thirds of Americans believe there are few, if any, absolute truths to direct human behavior.

Barely half of Lutherans, Methodists, and Presbyterians believe in Satan, but 56 percent of Lutherans and 49 percent of Methodists believe in UFOs. One-third of Methodists and Presbyterians have faith in astrology. While nearly three-fourths of all Americans believe in hell, hardly any believe it to be their likely destination in eternity.[20]

Historian Thomas C. Reeves reflects that Christianity in modern America is, in large part, innocuous:

It tends to be easy, upbeat, convenient, and compatible. It does not require self-sacrifice, discipline, humility, and otherworldly outlook, a zeal for souls, a fear as well as love of God. There is little guilt and no punishment, and the payoff in heaven is virtually certain.[21]

Does it matter that religious faith is fuzzy and failing? Clearly. Faith has consequences. People act according to their beliefs. If they are uncertain, they will act without confidence or not at all. In Herberg's time, although the content of personal faith in America was anemic, there was yet a society-wide consensus that religious faith supports the American way of life. Today the perennial American Dream of a just society and the good life for every citizen is in jeopardy, because the erosion of religious faith has weakened community and replaced it with self-indulgence.

It is no coincidence that the Dream was initially expressed in religious terms by the Puritan John Winthrop in 1630 in a sermon delivered aboard the ship *Arabella* on its voyage to the New World. It was reprised by yet another religious leader, Dr. Martin Luther King Jr. Addressing the future leaders of the Massachusetts Bay Colony, Winthrop warned our ancestors:

> We must consider that we shall be a city upon a hill. The eyes of all people are upon us, so that if we deal falsely with our God in this work we have undertaken, and so cause Him to withdraw His present help from us, we shall be made a story and a byword through the world.[22]

On the steps of the Lincoln Memorial 333 years later, Dr. King spoke of this "city on a hill" in more personal terms:

I have a dream that my four little children will one day live in a nation where they will not be judged by the color of their skin, but by the content of their character.[23]

Our nation's destiny was established from the outset on faith in God's favor toward us and on our responsibilities to one another. To remain faithful we need to be reminded from time to time of our blessings and mutual obligations, and to deepen our faith. As historian Daniel J. Boorstin describes the original vision of America:

> The beacon for misguided mankind was to be neither a book nor a theory. It was to be the community itself. America had something to teach all men: not by precept but by example, not by what it said but by how it lived.[24]

The Faith We Still Profess

Early each day my Scottish terrier and I are silent witnesses to a lingering expression of traditional American faith. As we take our morning constitutional on the playing fields of an elementary school near our Virginia home, the school's public address system carries the voices of first graders reciting the Pledge of Allegiance. Years ago, as a schoolchild, I too began class each day, hand over heart, promising fidelity to the land of my birth.

The Pledge of Allegiance is a civic prayer that comes naturally to a diverse nation whose trust in God is affirmed even on its currency. That confidence consists of more than mere patriotism. We share the conviction—whether we were born here or arrived only recently—that we are blessed as Americans and enjoy a common covenant with our creator. If anything, our nation's representatives in Congress take their civic obligations even more devoutly than our schoolchildren: they start each day with prayers invoking God's participation in their deliberations.

The American pledge of faith is unique among nations. British journalist Jeremy Paxman confesses that "no English person can look at the swearing of allegiance that takes place in American schools every day without feeling bewilderment: that sort of public demonstration of patriotism seems so, well, naive."[25]

Inevitably, all firmly-held faiths appear naive to outsiders. As a graduate student in Paris in the 1960s, I was introduced to a young black African who had composed the national anthems of a handful of newly-independent nations on his continent. One evening one of my fellow students, a young Catholic priest from Upper Volta, dragged out his portable phonograph to play his composer-friend's national anthems for me. His pride was infectious, as the young composer sang in tongues I could not understand to music that celebrated the faith of the new nations.

The religious faith that supports the American Dream encompasses our common aspirations, including employment, security, heath, education, opportunity, and the pursuit of happiness. It's likely that they don't realize it yet, but the first graders at my local elementary school are pledging allegiance to a dream they will pursue throughout their lives.

"Under God"

The recent erosion of religious faith in America is reflected in a court ruling that would delete the phrase "under God" from the Pledge of Allegiance, transforming it into a purely secular oath. Were he still among the living, the Reverend George Docherty would protest loudly. It was he who lobbied successfully to have that phrase added to the Pledge in 1954. Docherty was an immigrant clergyman, the Scottish-born pastor of the New York Avenue Presbyterian Church, a Washington, D.C., landmark a few blocks from the White House. He believed his adopted country to be founded on religious faith.

Docherty and I met occasionally in the old Washington studios of WTTG-TV, where we alternated providing the five-minute inspirational segments that opened and concluded that station's broadcast day. For years, our little sermons served as bookends on Channel Five's regular programming—reminders that television itself, then a relatively recent addition to the American Dream, stemmed from the same source of national faith. In the late 1950s and early 1960s, before the nation's religious decline, Docherty and I talked a lot about faith, gratitude, and responsibility in these United States.

Docerty affirmed that common cause and common consent rest on a common faith, however shallow and inarticulate. America's conviction (some would call it the American conceit) is that we as a people are singularly blessed: that like the Israelites of old, we are a chosen people. In the words of our unofficial National Anthem:

America, America,
God shed his grace on thee
And crowned thy good with brotherhood . . .

Our national poet, Walt Whitman, said more:

I say that the real and permanent grandeur
of these states must be their religion.
—"Starting from Paumanok," *Leaves of Grass*, 1900

But Reverend Docherty insisted that grace creates obligation: that Americans are required to respond to God's generosity by sharing our bounty and building community.

Despite the precipitous decline and softening of faith among individual Americans, the United States remains one of the most religious nations on the face of the earth. The statistics of religious faith in America are still staggering. No other nation approaches them. Ninety-five of every one hundred Americans acknowledge God. Three-fourths of us admit to praying every day of our lives, and most of us insist that our prayers are answered (although not necessarily the way we asked them to be).[26]

Nevertheless, our mile-wide, inch-deep faith is more vulnerable than many religious Americans would care to admit. Hope is fragile, and love is always in shorter supply than needed. Not everyone shares in the American Dream or the foundation of faith it is built upon. There is much unfinished business, and this is as good a time as any to set about completing our forefathers' city upon a hill.

Chapter 2

The
Virtues
and
Vices
of
Diversity

"The nation with the soul of a church."
—G. K. Chesterton

VISITORS TO THESE SHORES ARE AMAZED THAT AMERICAN churches advertise in the Yellow Pages. It's not because our houses of worship are businesses, of course. With the exception of the odd televangelist, American religion is noncommercial. But we have so many churches that they constitute a marketplace of faith, and the selection must be displayed somewhere. In our modest Virginia county phonebook, squeezed between ads for chiropractors and cinemas, are listings for nearly two hundred churches.

To help negotiate this thicket of faith, the denominations are broken down alphabetically. In the *A* section alone there are African-Methodist Episcopal churches, African-Methodist Episcopal Zion congregations, All Denominations, Apostolic churches, and Assemblies of God. In our churchgoing county there are sixty-five Baptist churches alone, including Independent and Southern Baptist Convention. The local Baha'i Faith congregation has managed to slip into the church directory as well, while synagogues and mosques have their own listings.

At the moment, Quakers, Adventists, Jehovah's Witnesses, and Buddhists must travel to adjacent counties to worship, but our Mormons are long since well established. Altogether, we have more places of worship in Prince William County than we have schools, banks, libraries, auto dealers, cinemas, and restaurants combined!

Visitors to the United States are stunned by this smorgasbord of faith, whereas we Americans take our religious diversity (like our ethnic and cultural diversity) for granted. From our colonial beginnings, the Latin motto *E Pluribus Unum* has remained the formula for what is still an immigrant nation: From many, one. We share common values and pursue the identical dream, but the melting pot does not extend to our expressions of religious faith. Lamentably, while our faiths are diverse, they are not deep. We believe without being able to articulate our beliefs.

A Nation without a Reformation

Dietrich Bonhoeffer, who was martyred for his faith by the Nazis, noted that America, unlike Europe, has never required a Reformation, because we have no established church to rebel against. Long ago we contrived a government that respects religion without favoring any particular faith. When religious reform is needed in America, it is typically accomplished locally, denomination by denomination, congregation by congregation.

Today, at the dawn of the third Christian millennium, there are as many as one thousand denominations in the United States. But even at the very outset there was diversity. Among the English-speaking colonists, there were the Puritans in New England and the Anglicans in Virginia. On the West Coast were Spanish-speaking Catholics, joined by French-speaking coreligionists in the North and Middle West. And, lest we forget, Native Americans had their own faiths.

With so much variety, one might expect vigorous competition among the faiths. Happily, despite significant dogmatic and institutional differences, we find cooperation and collaboration. In Prince William County, Virginia, we have thriving ministerial associations in both ends of the county, joining clergy of many denominations in mutual support of their individual ministries. In addition we have a huge nondenominational chapel used for interfaith worship and sharing. In recent years, when racial tension, drugs, and crime were tearing at the fabric of our community life and threatening our safety, our county government asked the churches to take the lead in combating prejudice and violence. It was not collusion of church and state, but only a recognition that citizens and churchgoers share the same values.

But if religious congregations in America get along so well, why do they remain autonomous? To put it another way, if they are basically expressing the same core faith, why do they so relish their differences?

One Easter back in the late '60s, when I was the editor of the West Hartford, Connecticut, newspaper, I asked each person on my staff to attend a different church in our town, then report back about the sermons being preached to our community. It has been stated that Americans are never so segregated as we are on Sunday morning, so I wondered if our Catholics, Lutherans, Congregationalists, Episcopalians, Baptists, and other congregations were hearing different messages. Not at all, we learned and duly reported. Without prior consultation, each priest and minister proclaimed the redemption of mankind. Each fixed on the faith all Christians share.

The Public Religion

Of course, one of the reasons we have so many denominations is because our parents and grandparents brought them with them when they came here. Religious preferences are largely a matter of habit and culture, not theology. We are comfortable with what we know, even when we know very little. In matters of faith and practice, one size does not fit all Americans.

Accordingly, Catholics, Jews, and Muslims in our armed services are provided by the government with chaplains of their own faith. But it would be impossible to serve all Protestant servicemen and women with uniformed clergy from their own denominations. Happily, few Protestants complain. They are grateful for a government that acknowledges the faith needs of those who defend our nation.

In recent years I was privileged to serve on the governing board of Washington National Cathedral, one of the most magnificent houses of worship in America. American statesmen and women are buried there. Although governed and maintained by the Episcopal Church, the cathedral wisely offers itself as a home for all faiths. In the absence of an established American church, that is the only possible role for a church that calls itself "national."

But smaller churches across America, regardless of denomination, also devote themselves to the public as community resources, welcoming everyone regardless of creed. From Monday through Saturday a typical church building is home to 12-step programs, Boy Scouts and Girl Scouts, Big Brothers and Big Sisters, and an array of organizations that are not religious in nature but that help individuals and groups in the community pursue the American Dream. That is practical ecumenism.

Early in our history as a nation, de Tocqueville acknowledged a treasure that he called "civil religion" and that Thomas Jefferson called the "general religion."[1] This is a national creed that distills values common to all sects, among all religions, and across all cultures. De Tocqueville and Jefferson would be bewildered by the variety of religious faiths proclaimed in millennial America, but satisfied that Americans maintain a common faith that, although typically inarticulate, is nonsectarian. Religious denominations remain divided by questions of doctrine, worship, and revelation. But what they agree on drives the American Dream. This public faith infuses American life with a sense of transcendence and joint destiny. Although every American profits from this faith, no one is forced to assent to it. Nevertheless, as our founders predicted, the constitutional order and American civilization depend on it.

In a handwritten account, the Reverend Ethan Allen recorded this encounter with Jefferson, which illustrates the public faith:

> President Jefferson was on his way to church of a Sunday morning with his large red prayer book under his arm when a friend, querying him after their mutual "Good morning," he said, "Which way are you walking, Mr. Jefferson?" To which he said, "To church, sir." "You going to church, Mr. J.? You do not believe a word of it." "Sir," said Mr. J., "no nation has ever existed or been governed without religion. Nor can be. The Christian religion is the best religion that has ever been given to man, and I as chief magistrate of this nation am bound to give it the sanction of my example."[2]

A Faith That Makes Us Free

De Tocqueville noted that, whereas religion in Europe had kept citizens in bondage, it was teaching Americans to be free:

> There is an innumerable multitude of sects in the United States. They are all different in the worship

they offer to the Creator, but all agree concerning the duties of men to one another. Each sect worships God in its own fashion, but all preach the same morality in the name of God. . . . What is most important for (society) is not that all citizens should profess the true religion, but that they should profess religion.[3]

The French visitor noted that clergy in the United States were at pains to refrain from active participation in government and political parties. In America, religion, he believed, does not influence government directly "but it does direct mores, and by regulating domestic life it helps to regulate the state."[4] In short, Americans' common faith tells us how to behave.

Abraham Lincoln was the rare president who belonged to no church, yet his invocation of the nation's public faith was eloquent. In the midst of the Civil War he proclaimed a day for "national prayer and humiliation," proposing that "it is the duty of nations as well as men to own their dependence upon the overruling power of God [and] to confess their sins and transgressions in humble sorrow." His proclamation of a National Fast-Day for March 30, 1863, reads like a sermon:

We have been preserved, these many years, in peace and prosperity. We have grown in numbers, wealth, and power as no other nation has ever grown; but we have forgotten God. We have forgotten the gracious hand which preserved us in peace, and multiplied and enriched and strengthened us; and we have vainly imagined, in the deceitfulness of our hearts, that all these blessings were produced by some superior wisdom and virtue of our own. Intoxicated with unbroken success, we have become too self-sufficient to feel the necessity of redeeming and preserving grace, too proud to pray to the God that made us. It behooves us, then, to humble ourselves before the offended Power, to confess our national sins, and to pray for clemency and forgiveness.[5]

If no chief executive since Lincoln has assumed the role of chastising prophet, it is not for lack of a national faith that binds all Americans in conscience to their creator and to one another.

Freedom of Conscience

Religious diversity in America stems from more than mutual tolerance. Early in the new nation's history, James Madison feared that should religion be "kindled into enthusiasm," it might "become a motive to persecution and oppression." Happily, that has not come to pass. When Patrick Henry proposed taxing Americans for the "annual support of the Christian religion," James Madison opposed it, arguing, "Whilst we assert for ourselves a freedom to . . . observe the religion which we believe to be of divine origin, we cannot deny an equal freedom to those whose minds have not yet yielded to the evidence which has convinced us."[6]

Freedom of conscience is the first of our liberties, requiring respect for the rights of all others. As William J. Bennett has noted:

Religious beliefs do deserve, in our time, common acknowledgment, mutual respect, and public encouragement. The Founders saw no conflict between our individual rights and our common values. In their minds, complete neutrality between particular religious beliefs can and should coexist with public acknowledgment of general religious values.[7]

Despite freedom of individual belief, religion in America has never been a private concern only. Our shared *public* values are based on faith. For want of a religious foundation, other democracies have failed to establish freedom through consensus. It is worth noting that, although secular humanists identify religion with superstition, they nevertheless retain and promote the values founded on faith.

When then-Minnesota Governor Jesse Ventura rapped organized religion as a "sham and a crutch for weak-minded people who need strength in numbers,"[8] he missed the point that religious faith, expressed in numbers, is precisely what makes Americans good citizens. When the governor added that religion "tells people to go out and stick their noses in other people's business,"[9] he was blind to the fact that it is only through shared values and common consent that Americans are able to live at peace with one another.

It is not surprising, then, that a 1996 Barna Research Group poll revealed that 85 percent of Americans believe Christians and other practicing believers have a positive effect on our society, whereas only 13 percent believed that atheists improve our national life. It may well be that the faith Americans possess in common is actually stronger, or at least better articulated, than the faith they share with their coreligionists in church on Sunday. The Barna poll concluded that, at century's end, "the new perception of religion [is] a personalized, customized form of faith views which meets personal needs, minimizes rules and absolutes, and which bears little resemblance to the 'pure' form of any of the world's major religions."[10]

In short, there is less that separates the religious beliefs of Americans than is suggested by the proliferation of our denominations and sects. We may in fact have achieved the ecumenical ideal without realizing it, but by paying the heavy price of vagueness and syncretism that cannot support commitment.

The Reality of Religious Life in America

In the new century, Americans who are still religious no longer confine the practice of their faith to their churches. Many are more active in what can only be classified as "parachurches," such as Youth for Christ, Young Life, the Billy Graham Evangelistic Association, and television's *700 Club*. Every week denominational religion is giving ground to independent congregations, interdenominational community churches, and even interfaith worship and service groups.

De Tocqueville recognized the American penchant for creating communities of interest. The need to seek common expression of our private faiths is overwhelming. As Phyllis A. Tickle affirms:

> The common denominator . . . is the American conviction that private faith . . . must find corporate

expression and communal exercise to be real. The interdenominational or even the interfaith union gives us a means through which to realize and effect the universal theology of hope, faith, and brotherhood that we hold, however diversely, in common. It worships and expresses and is active in the name of the God we reference as ground zero . . . without requiring that any one of us declare . . . either the particulars or the certainty of God.[11]

In short, the faith held by individual Americans is typically a personal theology, privately forged, rather than a detailed assent to creed or catechism. Today our faiths develop through reading, conversation, seminars, rallies, and retreats, and are honed on individual experience. Increasingly, they are not systematized, dogmatized, or organized by anyone else. They are at once provisional and strongly-held, inconsistent yet pragmatic. The faith we forge today is the one with which we confront life tomorrow. In the past, when faith faltered, Americans merely adjusted their beliefs; today many are prone to jettison religion altogether.

The faithful move among the nation's denominations, typically prompted by disagreement and disenchantment as well as by personal conflict. A young adult will change churches simply because a different denomination provides him or her with a cadre and a social life. As well, Americans move between faith communities because of interfaith marriage.

Intermarriage is viewed with some alarm by Jews and Catholics, but is also a problem for Protestants. Once a couple has children, a choice must be made whether the father's or mother's church will be the family's faith home. Often Protestant couples "split the difference" and find another denomination they find congenial, or they drop out altogether.

Jews and Catholics who marry those of other faiths enjoy no easier solution. Rabbis have warned for years that interfaith marriage, if unimpeded, will destroy observant Judaism in America. The number of Muslim Americans is overtaking our Jewish population, and Islam will soon be the nation's second faith.

Although Catholics comprise one-fourth of all Americans, interfaith marriage (as well as divorce) threatens to erode the number of practicing Catholics. Nearly half of all Catholic men born in the 1950s married women of other faiths. Intermarriage among Catholics is double what it was before the Second Vatican Council in the 1960s.[12]

Breaking Away, Binding Together

In the mile wide, inch deep world of faith, we cannot be certain whether the pull of church unity or the push of dissent is the stronger force in America. One thing is clear: the ecumenical movement seeks *communion* among the denominations, not the formation of a single church. Whereas Martin Luther prompted the breakup of the Christian church about five centuries ago, his followers are leading the movement to rejoin the churches.

In the last year of the old century the Evangelical Lutheran Church in America voted for "full communion" with the Episcopal church, the Presbyterian church, the Reformed church, the United Church of Christ, and the Moravian church. They did not vote for a merger, but for mutual recognition of each others' sacraments, sharing of ministers, and institutional cooperation. In short, they respect each other and will work together without giving up their distinctive liturgies, doctrines, and cultures. Such arrangements represent American pragmatism and good will at their best: much gained, nothing lost.

A new generation of clergy is being trained to serve the larger church through their own denominations. I sit on the board of the Washington Theological Consortium, a confederation of Catholic and Protestant seminaries from Gettysburg, Pennsylvania, to Richmond, Virginia, including houses of study that train ministers for African-American congregations. The seminaries have combined their library resources and their course offerings, and their faculties join frequently to learn from each other. Every student is required to take courses at other seminaries in different faith traditions. The intent is to deepen one's own faith understanding by confronting it with the faith understanding of others.

When I joined the board, I asked whether the seminaries risked losing their students to another denomination represented in the consortium. Our chairman laughed, and replied, "Not likely. Each denomination has so many requirements for ordination, leaving little temptation to start all over again elsewhere." In creating a national forum to bring the churches to bear on social and political issues on which they agree, the consortium is proving that faith can be both diverse *and* deep.

The fabric of faith in America resembles Joseph's coat of many colors: beautiful in its diversity. But there are occasional rips in the fabric. The Reverend John A. Cherry broke from the African Methodist Episcopal

Zion Church in 1999. A former furniture salesman, Cherry admits that as a young man he used drugs and jeopardized his marriage. But in 1981 he had a conversion experience and founded the Full Gospel AME Zion Church.

From twenty-four members meeting in a storefront in Suitland, Maryland, his congregation grew until he now has a megachurch with two chapels serving twenty-four thousand members and a private Lear jet for his travels. In addition, about twenty-five to thirty independent congregations look to him for leadership. Cherry was introduced to the nation by President Clinton in his 1995 State of the Union address, honored for his church's programs to strengthen marriage and family life. But he ran afoul of the denomination's hierarchy when he took to ordaining ministers, healing, and teaching congregants to speak in tongues.

In a massive ceremony in 1999 that lasted four hours and featured an orchestra and massed choir, Cherry was consecrated as leader of a new group of ministers splitting from their two-hundred-year-old denomination. "Are you born of God's Spirit and filled with his Spirit, with evidence of speaking in tongues?" he was asked. "Are you fully persuaded that you have been called into this office according to the will of our Lord Jesus Christ?" Cherry replied, "I am fully persuaded."[13]

Thus another denomination was launched and the AME Zion church weakened. Assuming the powers of a bishop, Cherry justified the schism by appealing to freedom of conscience and predicted that "scores of other churches and ministries will now experience the liberty that Christ has promised us."

The Next Church

With the notable exception of the Baptists, most mainstream Protestant denominations in America have been suffering serious membership erosion for decades. This slippage is not necessarily an indication of a permanent rejection of faith and practice, however, but of a shift favoring evangelical and pentecostal churches, and nondenominational megachurches.

Incidentally, despite the attention paid by the news media, there is little evidence of a resurgence of fundamentalism favoring the so-called Religious Right. Polls indicate that no more than one in ten Republican voters embrace the full agenda of the Christian Coalition. In fact, 86 percent of the conservative Southern Baptist Convention reject it. Only 6 percent of all Americans hold to the literal interpretation of the Scripture and are *at the same time* opposed to abortion, premarital sex, and homosexuality in all cases. The rest of us have different mixtures of convictions. In matters of faith and conscience Americans remain rugged individualists.[14]

"The Next Church" is the name commentator Charles Trueheart gives to the burgeoning independent, entrepreneurial congregations that are attracting many Baby Boomers back to religion in the new millennium: "No spires. No crosses. No robes. No clerical collars. No hard pews. No kneelers. No biblical gobbledygook. No prayer by rote. No fire, no brimstone. No pipe organs. No dreary 18th century hymns. No forced solemnity. No Sunday finery. No collection plates."[15]

Frankly, Trueheart's description would fit my own Quaker meeting house in Virginia, now over a century and a half old, with about 120 adult members. But he is describing brand new churches, some of which draw as many as ten thousand people on a weekend. There are as yet not many more than a thousand of them in a nation of four hundred thousand churches, but they are the fastest-growing congregations in America.

Their power to attract and serve stems, in part, from their size. Consider that half the nation's churches have fewer than seventy-five members. Accordingly, they can do little more than offer a time and a place for worship and some mutual support. These churches are dying at the rate of fifty every week in America.

But the new nondenominational megachurches are also endowed with a critical mass, big budgets, operating efficiencies, and huge volunteer pools, enabling them to diversify and offer what Trueheart calls "new product lines" to meet their congregations' needs. No one quite knows what to call these new churches, because they are independent of one another and rarely share in the traditions of the mainline Protestant faiths. They are called full-service churches, pastoral churches, apostolic churches, "new tribe" churches, seeker-sensitive churches, even shopping-mall churches. Unlike mainline churches, they are not named after Jesus, his mother, or the saints.

Kenton Beshore, the senior pastor of Mariners Church in Newport Beach, California, says of his massive congregation, "We give them what they want, and we give them what they didn't know they wanted—a life change."[16] That change is facilitated by a community of mutual service. Mariners and churches like it assume the roles of Welcome Wagon, the USO, the Rotary, the quilting bee, the coffee shop, the mixer, the family, and the school.

In Trueheart's words, they "convey membership in a community, with its benefits of friends and solace and purpose, and the deep satisfaction of service to others."[17] As communities crumble, jobs are down-sized, and government shrinks from social responsibility, the churches are left to take up the slack. But relatively few of them are large and strong enough to do the job. Hence the megachurch.

Of Business and Customers

The new churches are notoriously businesslike, and even business guru Peter Drucker admires their management. Texas businessman Bob Buford says that the new churches address the same questions as any entrepreneur entering the marketplace: What is our business? Who is our customer? What does the customer consider value?[18] If God appears to be missing from these considerations, it is only because the new entrepreneurial pastors consider God a *given* who can be relied on if humans do their part. They consider it their job to create church structures that encourage their flocks to be faithful to the two great commandments: To love God and neighbor, and to find some life satisfaction in the process.

The new churches either defy diversity or simply ignore it, content to dispense with creeds and traditions in favor of serving their congregants' needs. To the question, What is our business? They answer: To develop fully devoted followers of Christ. As for their customers, they are overwhelmingly Baby Boomers (born between 1946 and 1964) along with their families. By and large, these adults are economically comfortable but personally and socially disenchanted. So, instead of sermons, they are offered "messages" aimed at inspiring and motivating them to faith and service.

In at least one respect, the megachurches are like their more traditional Reformation counterparts: they tend to attract like-minded people who are racially and economically compatible. So they are no better at solving the problem of America being racially segregated on Sunday. Still, they aim not only to satisfy the souls of their members, but to engage them in serving the secular community. That is progress.

The new churches shun pulpits and hymnals in favor of overhead projectors. Their liturgies tend to include personal testimonials and dramatic sketches. Their altars are often only symbolic stage props, and communion services are consigned to special occasions. Music dominates their services, but do not expect Bach or Palestrina. Most "next church" music was composed within the past decade.

By favoring contemporary music, the megachurches are seeking unchurched people, especially those with children. Chuck Fromm, the chairman of Maranatha Music, who supplies such churches with contemporary praise and worship music, insists, "We better think about our sound and how we are reaching our community, or we will be the Amish of the twenty-first century."

In a time of religious decline the megachurches are successful. But are they authentic to the faith they represent? Leith Anderson, of Wooddale Church in Eden Prairie, Minnesota, argues that the way most Americans worship is not at all authentic, but culturally conditioned and a matter of comfortable habit. In his book, *A Church for the 21st Century*, he writes:

> While the New Testament speaks often about churches, it is surprisingly silent about many matters that we associate with church structure and life. There is no mention of architecture, pulpits, lengths of typical sermons, or rules for having a Sunday school. Little is said about style of music, order of worship, or times of church gatherings. There were no Bibles, denominations, camps, pastors' conferences, or board minute meetings. We don't know many details, and if we reproduced the ones we do know, we would end up with synagogues, speaking Greek, and the divisive sins of the Corinthians.[19]

Even smaller, more traditional churches now offer worship options. Some Episcopal churches, for example, schedule a traditional service, a contemporary service, and a charismatic service. Stanley Copeland of Pollard United Methodist Church in Tyler, Texas, offers his members a worship menu he calls, "vanilla, chocolate, and strawberry."[20] But for churches with only modest congregations, such options only serve to divide the faithful into even smaller cohorts.

When people walked to worship, the small neighborhood church had the virtue of convenience. Today the megachurches enjoy the same advantage over neighborhood churches that Wal-Mart has over the corner store. Americans are accustomed to driving distances for value. Buford explains, "People don't work in their neighborhoods. People don't shop in their neighborhoods. People don't go to the movies in their neighborhoods. So why should we expect them to go to church in their neighborhoods? They'll drive right by small churches to get to attend a larger one that offers more in the way of services or programs."[21]

A Free Market of Faith

Although the Episcopal church devoted the last decade of the twentieth century to evangelization, it not only failed to attract large numbers of the unchurched, but lost many long-term members and saw its total membership diminish. Like many of the mainstream Protestant denominations, it found itself caught up in intramural wrangling that had little to do with the spiritual and service lives of its rank-and-file members. Clashes over abortion, women priests, the ordination of gay clergy, and revisions of the prayer book and hymnal are diversions from any church's agenda.

By contrast, evangelical and Pentecostal churches, as well as independent megachurches, take a hard line on controversial issues or dismiss them as distractions for private debate. Either way, these churches are proving to be more attractive to unchurched Americans, who seek spiritual reassurance rather than religious controversy. One mainline pastor, Michael Foss, of Prince of Peace Lutheran Church in suburban Minneapolis, Minnesota, laments that controversies create divisions. He says:

I'm convinced you can be a Christian on either side of those issues. One of the tragedies of our culture is the tendency to draw lines where they needn't be drawn. Christians ought to stop throwing rocks at other Christians. We don't have to agree on everything. And these are side issues. What we're about is spiritual renewal.[22]

Religious diversity in America has created a vast marketplace of faith, where choices are made less for each denomination's dogma than for its determination to make members welcome, transform their lives, and put them to work serving others. Lest we confine the marketplace to Protestant Christians alone, consider what the Catholic church and Reform Judaism are doing.

The Catholic church tends to lose members not because they stop believing but because they have divorced and remarried. Today the church is making every effort to reincorporate lapsed Catholics into the church community and, where possible, to validate their second marriages. Increasingly, Catholics accept that artificial contraception, though condemned by the church, is a private matter and no barrier to a full faith life.

Reform Judaism, once prized for not insisting on strict traditions and practices, now senses that it is those very traditions that give its members a sense that they are a people apart. So, without insisting, Reform rabbis are nevertheless challenging their members to observe the Sabbath, to learn Hebrew, to keep fasts, and to pray on feast days. That challenge, they believe, will increasingly attract secular Jews to lives of religious observance.

In the American religious marketplace, diversity is often more apparent than it is real, but competition is rife to reclaim the religious dropouts to faith and practice. With doctrinal differences less a matter of contention than in centuries past, the challenge is to ensure that the individual faith of Americans is founded on more than mere sentiment, that it transforms us, and that it compels us to serve others.

Chapter 3

The
Faith
of
Positive
Thinking

"Not in the past or in the future,
but now and here is Heaven within us."
—Andrew Carnegie

ONLY IN AMERICA DO BUMPER STICKERS URGE MOTORISTS to "Honk if you love Jesus." Why wait, after all, for Gabriel to sound his horn, when we can lean on our own, proclaiming our faith from the driver's seat? In America, religious belief, where it still exists, is buoyant, its vitality undiminished since the Puritans set about building a New Jerusalem in Massachusetts and a shining "City upon a Hill" in the New World. The

American Dream of the good life, still shared by believers and secularists alike, rests on that persistent sense of destiny.

Not infrequently, however, enthusiasm takes on a life of its own, straining its religious roots. Although the Reverend Norman Vincent Peale served for more than half a century as senior pastor of the Reformed Church of America, relatively few Americans ever heard him preach at his Marble Collegiate Church in New York City. They knew him from his book, *The Power of Positive Thinking*, an enormous publishing success that sold more than fifteen million copies and was translated into forty-two languages. It mixed psychology with religion, promoting the principle that God helps those who help themselves.

Peale was unfairly reviled by his peers for reducing religious faith to strategies for worldly success. In fact, he retained the original Reformers' conviction that religious faith is, above all, confidence in God, and argued that all we need to add is confidence in ourselves.[1]

Ironically, that confidence did not come easy to Peale himself. The son of an itinerant Methodist preacher, he reported:

> I'm a tough case, and I had to be saved several times! I believe it is perfectly possible for a person to be saved once and for all, but let me tell you that human nature is bad, and the devil is very powerful, and he can get into the mind of anyone who does not have the Spirit in power to ward him off.[2]

In his ministry Peale insisted, "You've got to reach people on their own knowledge-level where they understand, and I think the average American is not educated in the terminology of the church as people were years ago." For two years he sought to bring a troubled man named Charlie to faith. Time and again, Charlie would reply, "I have half-a-mind to do that." Finally, in exasperation, Peale challenged him:

Charlie, I believe your trouble is that you're a "half-a-minder". . . . You'd like to be strong in your morals and in your faith, and you'd like to be effective in your business. But let me tell you, you'll never in the world reach any of those goals unless you go *all* out instead of just *half* out.[3]

With Charlie still unconvinced, Peale insisted that he could be saved by faith in the Savior who gave his life on the cross for the cantankerous, doubting man. Then:

The strangest look came over Charlie's face, and he fell to his knees and surrendered his life to the Lord Jesus Christ. He was transformed before my eyes. . . . It wasn't psychology that saved Charlie. It was the Lord Jesus Christ.[4]

Heaven on Earth

Alas, positive thinking is a solitary pursuit, whereas pursuing the American Dream is a common cause. If religious faith in America were marked by private enthusiasm alone, you and I (like Charlie) would seek only individual salvation, and there would be no faith or Dream to be shared. Instead, our struggle as a people to tame a continent forced us from the outset into communal enterprises, requiring faith in one another. Mutual dependency nurtured a shared faith in God and man, and in a common destiny.

From the outset, Americans of faith sought to create more than merely secular societies. Good people, our ancestors believed, ought to be able to make good communities. So, from the founding of the Massachusetts Bay Colony to the creation of present-day communes, their objective has been utopian—to create a facsimile of heaven on earth.

The persistent utopian impulse in America is most dramatically exemplified by the Mormons—Latter-Day Saints—who continue to surpass even the success of our Puritan forebears in constructing an earthly society based on spiritual faith. Founded on private revelations in the 1820s to Joseph Smith, an illiterate New York farm boy, Mormonism prompted a mass mid-nineteenth century migration of believers to Utah, and has since grown into a worldwide missionary enterprise.

With continued high birth and conversion rates, Mormonism adds one million believers every decade, while obligatory tithing ensures a solid financial foundation for the church. Moreover, the Mormon ethic encourages economic success. On a per capita basis, the Church of Jesus Christ of Latter-Day Saints is the richest church in the world. A church-sponsored welfare system ensures that no faithful Mormon will ever be poor.

One of the ironies of human society is that freedom flourishes only when citizens live within restraints. In the absence of self-restraint, people become the victims of anarchy, terror, and the rule of force. We each go our own way, and the community collapses. In our nation at the moment we have more citizens behind bars for antisocial behavior than any other industrialized democracy, leaving the rulekeepers to fashion a just society for themselves.

Happily, there is evidence that religious faith helps us keep the rules, which is one more reason for decrying the decline of faith. *Newsweek* reveals that the single most critical factor in keeping a young urban African American male from crime and incarceration is church attendance. Not employment, not income, not family stability, but an active religious faith.[5]

Sociologist Rosabeth Kanter reveals that the Mormons employ commitment mechanisms that ensure the survival of utopian experiments: centralized leadership, clear ideology and regulations, rules for entry, screening procedures, and a requirement that each member invest a great deal psychologically for the privilege of belonging. She writes:

> In contradistinction to the larger society, which is seen as chaotic and unplanned, utopian communities are characterized by conscious planning and coordination. . . . Events follow a pattern. . . . A utopian often desires meaning and control, order and purpose, and he seeks those ends explicitly through his community.[6]

Few of these mechanisms are operative among Americans of faith.[7]

Earlier in my life, I worked in Utah among the Latter-Day Saints and noted their success firsthand.

Critics will complain that Mormonism produced an imperfect paradise. Nevertheless, it is probably the closest approximation of the American Dream yet realized through faith.

The Quiet Enthusiasts

Taken to extremes, of course, utopian communities take on the characteristics of cults—closed, elite societies that demand total dedication and unquestioning obedience to the whims of their leaders. Whereas religious utopias enthusiastically seek the peaceable kingdom now, cults grimly anticipate a future Armageddon. Crazy cults continue to flourish because sensible attempts to build heaven on earth so often collapse when confronted with rebellious human nature.

In contrast to the Mormons, the Quakers do not proselytize, so their numbers remain modest. Moreover, their attempt to build heaven on earth is managed quietly, modestly, economically, and by inner inspiration rather than external authority. Yet they, too, have been successful over time in constructing the American Dream on a foundation of faith and service. Longtime victims of persecution themselves, the Quakers nevertheless exemplify the unflagging optimism of religion in America that has benefited us all. They call themselves Friends.

In contrast to most faithful Americans, Friends dispense with clergy and creeds, ceremonies and churches, songs and sacraments, in favor of undirected silent meetings in bare rooms. Convinced of the existence of an inner light shared by all mankind, they insist on the potential for good in human nature. They hold that the real proof of their enlightenment and total commitment to God is their service to humanity. So they aim not to build heaven on earth for themselves alone, but for everyone. Their humanitarian work in Europe after World War II received the Nobel Peace Prize.

In colonial America, Quaker William Penn planned his Pennsylvania as a "holy experiment." He made the native Indians equals under the law and refused to take up arms against them. Quaker colonists in Pennsylvania were the first to call for the abolition of slavery, and by 1776 no American Friend owned slaves. Later, Quaker John Bellers advanced the first practical schemes for ending poverty, providing public education, and treating criminals humanely. Susan B. Anthony fought successfully for women's suffrage and equality of the sexes, while Dorothea Dix battled for enlightened treatment of the mentally ill, and Mary Calderone successfully campaigned for sex education. All these contributions are fixtures of the American Dream that we have inherited even as our faith has faltered.

In the last century, Friends extended their utopian vision to the rest of the world as relief workers throughout developing nations, creating islands of peace in the midst of conflict. In 1938 the Quakers were the first to protest to the Gestapo about Nazi brutality to the Jews. Today in strife-torn Ireland they hold a single meeting uniting Quakers from the North and South in peace. Here at home, in pursuing the American Dream for everyone, they are unburdened by nostalgia, fear, elitism, dogma, and unreasonable expectations. In their quiet way, they mirror the enthusiasm, optimism, and positive thinking of religion in millennial America without its self-indulgence.

Collective Enthusiasm

Alas, most people of faith in America are not drawn to planned utopian communities. Nevertheless, they overwhelmingly choose to nurture their religious beliefs in the context of *community*, be it church, synagogue, mosque, or faith-based fellowship. In Europe, by contrast, people keep their faiths and doubts pretty much to themselves, shunning "organized religion."

Despite our mile-wide religious faith, most Americans maintain that religion (along with politics) is not a subject for polite conversation, because it threatens to set us at odds with one another. Accordingly, religious toleration is more highly valued than proselytism. Why argue about God when we can more profitably cooperate to share in his blessings?

The typical American's faith is driven not by theology and creed, but by personal conviction and shared optimism.[8] Even in an earlier era, when revivalist preachers sought to shame believers into virtue, it was always with the intention of converting them to hopeful expectation. Today, with faith a mile wide and an inch deep, less is preached about individual guilt and more about our collective shortcomings in sharing God's bounty and peace. Americans may be uncertain about the content of their faith, but not about its mood, which is relentlessly upbeat.

For America, Peale preached a faith that moves mountains. "Our fathers," he declared, "handed down to us a prosperous and happy country. They said, 'We built this country on certain principles, see ye to it; remain faithful.'"[9] Peale was fond of quoting St. Paul ("I am ready for anything through the strength of the one who lives within me" [Philippians 4:13]) and Jesus himself ("Everything is possible to the man who believes" [Mark 9:23]).

Today, Robert H. Schuller, founder and pastor of California's Crystal Cathedral, echoes Peale's upbeat, activist faith. He, too, quotes Paul ("I leave the past behind, and with hands outstretched to whatever lies ahead, I go straight for the goal—my reward being the honor of being called by God in Christ [Philippians 4:13-14]) and Jesus ("Anyone who puts his hand to the plough and then looks behind him is useless for the kingdom of heaven" [Luke 9:62]).[10]

Billy Graham, perhaps the most respected evangelist of the twentieth century, was careful to temper his enthusiasm with a sober sense of the fragility of human nature. Yet, he too extracted optimism from Scripture, quoting St. Peter about Jesus ("Even now he brings you a joy that words cannot express, and which has in it a hint of the glories of Heaven" [1 Peter 1:8]).

Of course, one expects enthusiasm from evangelical Christians, but among American Catholics and Jews we also discover an accentuation of the positive that is peculiar to American faith. The late Archbishop Fulton J. Sheen was fond of quoting St. John ("I leave behind with you—peace; I give you my own peace, and my gift is nothing like the peace of this world" [John 14:27]).[11]

Similarly, when Rabbi Harold Kushner was moved by the premature death of his son to write his book, *When Bad Things Happen to Good People*, he sounded a note of optimism. Kushner argues that God imposed limitations on himself when he imbued nature with laws and humans with freedom. Still, he insists:

God has created a world in which many more good things than bad things happen. . . . Most people wake up on most days feeling good. Most illnesses are curable. Most airplanes take off and land safely. Most of the time, when we send our children out to play, they come home safely. The accident, the robbery, the inoperable tumor are life-shattering exceptions, but they are very rare exceptions.[12]

Moreover, Kushner suggests, life's tragedies are often blessings in disguise because they can spur human solidarity. "God," he says, "helps by inspiring people to help."[13]

The Collective Dream

American political leaders tend to agree on the shape of the national Dream, differing only on how best to achieve it: through government assistance or personal effort, with freedom or constraint. Religious leaders look beyond a temporal Dream to eternity, but agree on the imperative to build the kingdom on earth, where all may share God's bounty. Entrepreneurs abound, of course, feathering their own nests. Still, Americans of faith sense that the Dream can only be achieved collectively. "Hell," the Rev. Kenton Beshore preaches, "is a gated community," eliciting nervous laughter from many of the members of his California congregation who live in just such exclusive enclaves. "If you become a little private gated community . . . you're not going to be generous; you're going to live in fear." Jesus, he tells his mostly-affluent members, "tears down walls between you and the community."[14]

Utopias disappear because their founders fail to realize the extent of selfishness in human nature and our resistance to being restricted by rules. But an informal balance has been struck in American religious life, whereby fellowship and generosity go hand in hand. You might even say that generosity has become the price of fellowship. If, after all, in their isolation, people need the company of God and one another, they feel duty-bound to love God and help neighbors in need.

Most private philanthropy in the United States still goes to religious organizations, which in turn direct a large portion of their members' generosity to the needy, regardless of creed. Moreover, a majority of Americans of faith, from teens through adults, volunteer their time to assist the less fortunate, mostly through their churches.

This generosity rests on a personal faith that is confident and optimistic, whatever its depth or consistency. Revivalist D. L. Moody expressed that confidence more than a century ago. "Some day," he said, "you will read in the papers that D. L. Moody of East Northfield is dead." He continued:

Don't believe a word of it. At that moment I shall be more alive than I am now. I shall have gone higher, that is all; gone out of this old tenement of clay into a house that is immortal; a body that death cannot touch, that sin cannot taint, a body like unto His own glorious body. I was born of the flesh in 1837. I was born of the spirit in 1854. That which is born of the flesh may die. That which is born of the spirit will live forever.[15]

The "Cash Value" of Faith

The great American psychologist William James noted famously that religion has "cash value," meaning that it gives us answers and makes us feel more confident.[16] The entertainment industry, fearful to be accused of irreverence, has never known quite how to realistically depict lives of faith, but that has not stopped Hollywood from churning out biblical epics that deliver profits at the box office.

Nor has it prevented stars from wearing their faiths on their sleeves. Jane Russell, who challenged the production codes in the 1940s with her on-screen sexuality, became a born-again Christian and maintained that "the man upstairs" was "a livin' doll." Later, Shirley MacLaine became the high priestess of New Age faith, whose practitioners concentrate on self-realization.

Critics may object to equating New Age thinking with religion, but its practitioners treat it with the same reverence and enthusiasm as traditional faith, if not with the same sense of mutual responsibility. In fact, many Americans of faith combine New Age thinking with their conventional creeds because it is optimistic. Visit any large bookstore and you will find a section devoted to New Age that rivals the space accorded to religion.

More than twenty years ago Marilyn Ferguson published *The Aquarian Conspiracy,* which has since become the movement's unofficial bible. Ferguson predicted a new era of harmony and peace whose onset could be hastened simply by our being aware of its inevitability.

New Age is more a matter of attitude than creed or practice. It seeks development of one's human potential.

How that is achieved—be it by meditation, exercise, psychology, or herbal remedies—is not important, nor do New Agers cavil about what form one's fulfillment takes (serenity, sex, money, power—all are equally valid). What matters is knowing that personal potential is there, then exploiting it.

There is no God in the New Age church, unless it is the believer. MacLaine writes that, once you grasp that "you are God, you can create your own reality."[17] The Sermon on the Mount does not play well in the New Age, but positive thinking does. New Age optimism has no room for sin—only for failure to live up to one's personal potential.

The helpful lesson in New Age thinking is responsibility for oneself. Less attractive is the absence of any imperative to be responsible for one another. According to its canon, if your reality is unsatisfactory, there is no one to blame but yourself. If you are poor or sick or unattractive, it is your fault. Moreover, no one can plead that he or she is disadvantaged. Everyone is equally capable of becoming satisfied according to his or her own definition of bliss. Indeed, according to New Age thinking, everyone's lot will improve if each one of us begins to think positively.

Ferguson quotes de Tocqueville in favor of building a life of both spiritual and material success:

> If ever the faculties of the great majority of mankind were exclusively bent upon the pursuit of material objects . . . an amazing reaction would take place in the souls of some. I should be surprised if mysticism did not soon make some advance among people solely engaged in promoting its own worldly welfare.[18]

By this measure, material success comes first and affords the luxury of religious faith as an option. Whereas Americans traditionally have put faith first and trusted, by common effort and God's grace, to realize the American Dream of the good life.

"We find our individual freedom," Ferguson argues, "by choosing not a destination but a direction."[19] That direction is invariably *inward* and experiential. "Doctrine is losing its authority, and knowing is superseding belief,"[20] she argues. No longer is it enough to merely have faith in God; you must experience divinity.

Because of its optimism, New Age thinking appears to complement conventional religion, but is actually hostile to it. More than twenty years ago its Spiritual Counterfeits Project insisted that the New Age movement is "fundamentally hostile to Biblical Christianity," which recognizes sin and virtue, places constraints on behavior, and extols mutual responsibility. New Age thinking may be the American Dream become daydream. Only in a society as affluent as ours could the pursuit of happiness be considered the exclusive virtue.

The Two Faces of Optimism

At the outset of the twentieth century, religion was locked with science in a struggle to give ultimate meaning to life. A century later, most Americans have dismissed science's claim, because its explanations are too complex, tentative, and bloodless to satisfy. Science continues with success to address the "what" and "how" of life, but not the "why" and "what for"— the questions that most engage us. If the cosmos began with a Big Bang rather than with a creator's design, we are still left to determine our place in the universe. If the universe possesses no purpose, we are aliens in it, because human beings cannot act without purpose.

Today, in practical terms, science has become the handmaiden of technology, which surely makes living more comfortable (and even extends life), but which answers no ultimate questions. Science is disinterested—neither optimistic nor pessimistic. But people confronting their mortality are interested, and religion still serves that interest. As for moral decision-making, science has nothing to say.

Harvard theologian Harvey Cox likens science and religion to two tired boxers who have slugged away too long, reaching "an exhausted stalemate."[21] But in the course of the struggle, science has stripped traditional religion of some of its conceits. Most seminaries no longer bother to teach the traditional "proofs" for the existence of God, because the arguments have been discredited. Since Galileo, the churches can no longer pretend that the universe revolves around earth and man. Since Darwin, it has become vastly more difficult to define what it is about the human animal that exclusively bears God's image and likeness.

Moreover, scientific scholarship challenges believers' reliance on the Bible as a self-validating historical textbook. Increasingly, we realize that the Bible's truth is revealed in metaphor and story, and not because the story of creation, for example, can be proven as historical fact.

While religious faith still motivates a majority of Americans, it no longer rests on its old sturdy legs. Church, synagogue, and mosque can no longer prove what they preach, but they still offer believers the opportunity to *practice* what they preach—and to *experience* it. So, even in the absence of old certitudes, positive thinking reigns in religion.

Cox believes that the twenty-first century will be marked by the competition between religious fundamentalism and religious experientialism. Both movements are notable for their optimism. Both support the American Dream. But they are poles apart in what they seek. Fundamentalism aims to replace faith with certitude; experientialism aims to replace faith with the experience of the God within.

The Rewards of Positive Thinking

Historically, religious faith in America offers evidence that positive thinking, when linked with cooperative action, is effective, suggesting to believers that if they choose to be on God's side, he will be on theirs. To be sure, Martin Luther King Jr. was not given to the smug smiles we see on the faces of some televangelists, because his struggle was serious. Yet he made the secular movement for racial equality a holy mission, and he underscored religious faith as the foundation of the American Dream.

As yet, the ecumenical movement has barely affected the average churchgoer, because the typical Christian lacks both the knowledge and the interest to grapple with the doctrinal differences that still separate the churches.[22] In any case, individual congregations have disregarded those differences for decades, choosing to collaborate in ministry to the nation's needy regardless of faith. If American pragmatism is not analytical and profound (and it is not), it is nevertheless positive, good-natured, and effective.

There is every sign that, despite the decline of faith, positive thinking at the highest levels is also bearing fruit. With the Augsburg Accord, signed on Reformation Sunday in the final year of the old millennium, the Catholic and Lutheran churches formally agreed that the Protestant Reformation began with a misunderstanding that no longer need divide them. The Accord can only be interpreted positively: it has either fulfilled the original intent of the Reformation, or it has enrolled the more than one billion Catholics worldwide in a comprehensive and ongoing Reformation.

Either way, as the pope's representative affirmed at the time, "In the one Spirit we are all baptized into one body. Let us then pursue all that makes for peace and builds up our common life."[23]

The Augsburg agreement was yet another Catholic initiative to enter the new Christian millennium with a clean slate. Although signed in Germany, it represents American positive thinking and reflects the American Dream. In the waning years of the old millennium the pope not only apologized for the Inquisition and the persecution of Galileo, but also affirmed scientific evolution, and made overtures to the Orthodox church, to Islam, and to Judaism.

As the Augsburg Accord was being signed in Europe, church leaders in America joined in worship at Washington's National Cathedral, pledging their efforts toward reconstituting the one family of faith. Lutheran bishop Theodore F. Schneider pronounced it a "scandal that we tell husbands and wives to do things together and attend church together,"[24] when all members of the Christian family cannot find ways to share the same faith and ministry.

Lamentably, internal disputes within the mainstream denominations persist—notably about homosexuality and the role of women in the church—distracting those churches from the one faith and mission they share, prompting them to peer inward to hunt heresies, and encouraging dropouts from faith. Happily, the ecumenical movement appears to be strong enough to overcome (or at least bypass) any lingering parochialism. Whereas Peale once encouraged individual Americans to think positively, now the church as a whole is thinking that way about itself and its mission.

Strains in the American Faith

At the moment, the movement toward unity of faith and ministry is confined largely to the Catholic and mainline Protestant churches. But as Cox warns, American faith in the twenty-first century is likely to be dominated by movements that have agendas other than unity and service.[25] Fundamentalism and pentecostalism aim at *replacing* traditional faith with something its adherents consider more satisfying. Both movements are positive, to be sure, but neither gives thinking much credit. Both tendencies are well represented within the traditional churches as well as in their distinct faith communities.

The two strains share a common enthusiasm, but otherwise diverge. Whereas the traditional churches live comfortably within their creeds, sacraments, and liturgies, fundamentalists and pentecostals tend to regard this apparatus as mere convention. Instead, both movements prize something simpler and all-embracing, and they seek it passionately. For fundamentalists, the grail is *certainty*; for pentecostals, it is the *direct experience of God*. Any speculation about the future of faith in America and the impact of faith on the American Dream must take into account these two movements. Fundamentalism leaves no room for doubt. Indeed, uncertainty is considered a sin against confident faith, which alone guarantees salvation. Within the past century we have come to see that fundamentalism exists not only within Protestant Christianity, but within Judaism, Islam, Hinduism, Buddhism, and among those Catholics who decry the work of the Second Vatican Council.

What fundamentalists of all religious stripes share is a commitment to permanent revival and to the "fundamentals" of their faith, which Cox describes as "the non-negotiable bedrock beliefs of a religious tradition, which have undergone cultural erosion or direct attack by secular forces in the modern age."[26] Fundamentalists consider themselves to be besieged by a godless culture. Yet, intent on keeping their faith pure, they are more sensitive to rooting out heresy within their own faith communities than resisting unbelief in the world at large. Within every fundamentalist congregation there is a party line from which deviation is unacceptable.

Christian fundamentalism professes to defend the ancient truths underlying faith, but distorts them by treating them literally—insisting, for example, on the "inerrancy" of the Scriptures. Whereas Jesus was entirely comfortable teaching by means of parables, fundamentalists insist that every detail be historical and scientific. Positive thinking suffers from such mindless zeal.

Tongues on Fire

Increasingly, the passion that characterizes American religion has its source not in the acceptance of traditional creeds and the practice of piety, but in the individual's personal experience of God's love. Americans sense that to be alone with God is to be free. It is to feel God-like. To sense oneness with God requires no thinking, no study—only feeling. In times past and in other places the faithful were persuaded of the "otherness," the transcendence of God. But in America, optimism tends to domesticate the deity, even to obliterate the distinction between the human and the divine.

You cannot read Ralph Waldo Emerson, Joseph Smith, Mary Baker Eddy, or William James—each an American original—without sensing a confidence that is almost conceit. God is not distant, but a welcome presence. Of course, Jesus promised that if we but knock, the door will be opened. But Americans of faith tend to prefer a God who knocks, allowing them to decide whether to let him in.

Pentecostalism takes its name from an event, about fifty days after Jesus' resurrection, when his apostles received God's spirit of strength in tongues of fire and began to preach in strange tongues. It was the first revival meeting, and the preaching was practical. Its hearers understood the languages, even if the speakers didn't. Today, speaking in tongues is prized by pentecostals as a sign that God's spirit speaks through them. The problem is that no one understands what they are saying. One in five Americans claims to be a pentecostal, but only one in twenty-five claims to have spoken in tongues.

In any event, it is experience that matters. As we have noted, fundamentalism seeks to replace faith with certainty, but what could be more certain than to feel seized—even possessed—by God? Revivalists have long gloated that "a man with a doctrine doesn't stand a chance against a man with experience." In addition, pentecostalism seeks to revive the special gifts of healing and prophesy that marked the age of the apostles.

In addition to charismatic churches, there are charismatics operating within the traditional denominations, including Roman Catholicism. In recent years, the growth of pentecostalism has slowed among white people, but continues to accelerate among minorities and in developing nations. It is positive thinking that requires little thought-taking.

Early pentecostals believed that the kingdom of God was coming soon and designated themselves as its heralds. Aimee Semple McPherson drove in a car that carried the painted message: "Jesus Is Coming Soon: Get ready." But today's pentecostals have muted their apocalyptic warning, and are more inclined to preach the compassionate presence of God's Spirit as helper, healer, and companion. That message is likely to continue in the new century.

At the outset I quoted the quiet confidence of Andrew Carnegie, "Not in the past or in the future, but now and here is Heaven within us."[27] Pentecostal revivalism tends to be noisy, but the demand to replace faith with the experience of God's presence is as strong in a Quaker meeting house, where Friends sit in total silence awaiting the whisper of the Spirit to guide them.

People of faith clearly trust experience more than theology. Even the great twentieth-century theologian

Paul Tillich insisted that faith be subject to what he called "experiential verification." Still, the experience of God is not God himself, nor does the experience render the believer divine. Rather, faith must point to something beyond experience. Experience does not *create* God, but only *makes real* his existence and presence to the individual believer.

If replacing faith with certitude and experience results in pride and self-absorption, then the American Dream is in jeopardy. Doubt keeps believers humble, and true faith demands that they serve one another, rather than wallow in isolated self-assurance. If positive thinking is to continue to serve the Dream, the faithful must get out of themselves and into the world. The future of faith, and the Dream, depend on it.

Chapter 4

What's God Got to Do with It?

"My mind is my own church."
—Thomas Paine

EVERY YEAR THE FORMIDABLE *TIMES* OF LONDON SPONSORS A competition for the best sermon of the year. Competition is keen. Despite the fact that, on any given Sunday, fewer than one million Britons worship in that nation's official church, there is widespread curiosity about what is being preached from its pulpits. If recent prize sermons offer any indication, those messages are literate, decorous, sometimes uplifting, always consoling—but neither substantively nor distinctively

Christian. If the Son of God died on a cross to save mankind from its sins, you will seek in vain for that message in this pious, prizewinning rhetoric.

It was not surprising, then, that when the *Times* mischievously polled the nation's vicars in the mid-1990s, it discovered that the majority could not recall all of the Ten Commandments. Undaunted, one clergyman excused his memory lapse by insisting that people knew perfectly well how to behave decently as ladies and gentlemen without being constantly reminded of God's rules. In view of the fact that it is now estimated that fully half of male Britons will have spent some time in jail during the new century, the vicar may have been mistaken.

When the *Times* published its end-of-the-millennium list of the greatest people who have ever lived, it rated Jesus of Nazareth at the top. "All that we, at our best, still aspire to be," the newspaper proclaimed,

> is expressed in the Sermon on the Mount. That love of others might require our own death, that worldly success is as nothing when set against our inner humanity, that our lives are to be lived in a context of transcendent significance, these remain the highest human ideals.[1]

That is a fine little sermon in itself, and it came not from a pulpit but from a newspaper owned by the media mogul Rupert Murdoch, a man not celebrated for his piety.

Alas, you won't find that kind of thumbnail theology in American newspapers. Granted, at the same time, you are not likely to encounter clergy in the

United States who can't recall the Commandments. Still, there is a pervasive reluctance in America to rest religious faith on a firm foundation of scripture, creed, and morality. For many nominally faithful Americans, God has become an embarrassment to religion.

In recent decades there were breakaways as well as dropouts from faith. Traditional believers did not become less religious, but many from the mainline churches became disenchanted with secular accommodation and sought something stronger: the assurance of fundamentalism, the personal commitment of evangelicalism, the deep experience of pentecostalism. As the religious establishment favored liberal politics and social policy, the breakaways turned conservative, convinced that there was something important to conserve.

Religious Truth

Our nation's founders declared certain truths to be self-evident: the equality of men, as well as our right to life, liberty, and happiness—all pillars of the American Dream. Of course, there is no corresponding certitude in religion, which, while nourished by revelation, is nevertheless founded on faith.

Still, faith need not be as fragile and personal as bystanders might assume. In all the great religions, faith is founded on a bedrock of revelation, as well as the combined, consistent experience of billions of believers through the centuries. Whoever enters the world of faith—be it through church, temple, or mosque—is swept along on a tide of tradition that represents scholarship, morality, and occasional sanctity. In turn, the world of faith opens the life of grace. "Is it easy to love God?" C. S. Lewis was once asked. His response: "Yes, for those who do."[2] But it is even easier to ignore God or domesticate him.

Religious people act according to their beliefs, so faith and morality go hand in hand. When faith is fuzzy, behavior will suffer, and evil can lurk behind good intentions. Today's political correctness is only a cranky form of social etiquette. Morality is something else altogether. It requires service to others, and is seldom consoling. Love, the highest expression of morality, on occasion requires the sacrifice of one's own life.

Faith is more than feeling. Indeed, it is more than confidence in God. To have faith is to accept a personal relationship with God, but that relationship will be sentimental and complacent unless it is based on beliefs that can be expressed, shared, and tested, and that drive the way the believer behaves. To hold faith means to be faithful to the creator and to one another.

Lamentably, in recent decades the mainline churches have largely exchanged conviction for consolation and morality for good intentions. In an attempt to be relevant, they have become the captives of a complacent and agnostic culture. Increasingly, the faithful are indistinguishable in thought and behavior from the faithless. These days, to be dogmatic is to be considered narrow-minded; to be forceful in faith is to be considered presumptuous.[3] Unwittingly, the ecumenical movement has abetted the decline of dogma, because beliefs left unexpressed cannot provoke controversy and division. Silent churches keep the peace, but at what cost?

In academic circles, of course, skepticism is considered enlightened, but in public and private life agnosticism breeds anarchy. If character cannot be taught in our public schools, then it must come from parents and churches, assuming they are clear about their convictions. But Presbyterian, Methodist, and Episcopal churches lose nearly half of their young people forever, and close to half of Presbyterian boys and girls never return to any church.[4] Considering the rate of crime, violence, addiction, and teen pregnancy in the nation, the loss of practical faith among American youth is a recipe for disaster.

Faith and Churchgoing

Of course, Americans do not necessarily equate religious faith with churchgoing. Gallup polls reveal that overwhelming majorities of Americans, both churched and unchurched, agree that people "should arrive at their religious beliefs independent of any church or synagogue."[5] Wade Clark Roof and William McKinney add that, for Americans, "religious authority lies in the believer—not in the church, not in the Bible."[6] But consciences must be informed to be effective, prompting the teaching role of the churches—a role they increasingly abandon.

Even the Catholic church has moderated its preaching (if not its policy) in the face of resistance from its adherents. Gallup reports that more than two-thirds of Catholics rely on their consciences rather than church teaching in making difficult moral decisions. In practice, American Catholic majorities oppose the church on the issues of legalized abortion, contraception, and "safe-sex" education in the schools. According to Gallup, Catholic church attendance dropped from 74 percent in 1958 to 48 percent three decades later.[7]

What we have witnessed in the last twenty years is a steady decline in churchgoing after two centuries of rising attendance. On the eve of the American Revolution only 17 percent of Americans even belonged to churches. At the time of the Civil War one-third of Americans were church members, rising to half the nation at the turn of the twentieth century, and to two in three Americans in 1980.

Ironically, as membership increased, attendance declined. In 1993, when George Gallup Jr. asked Americans how often they worshiped together, 41 percent answered "every week." But in the same year two sociologists asked Americans to keep logs of how they actually spent their time during the week, without special reference to churchgoing. The diaries revealed that only 19.6 percent of Protestants and 28 percent of Catholics worshiped on any given Sunday.

A subsequent Barna poll indicated that the Sunday stay-at-homes are disproportionately Baby Boomers— 69 percent of whom sleep in on the Sabbath, followed by young adults eighteen to thirty years old, two-thirds of whom shun congregational worship altogether.[8]

Although the vast majority of Americans continue to believe in God, pray regularly, and identify a religious preference, only a minority now worship together regularly. What of the others? Their religious life, whether fervent or lackadaisical, is almost exclusively private and personal. Like Thomas Paine, their minds are their church.

Personal Religion

Nine of ten Americans believe that God cares for them on a personal and individual basis. Clearly, this is no longer the jealous God of wrath who spoke through burning bushes and clouds of locusts, but a kinder, gentler divinity who awaits his creatures' calls for assistance and invites intimacy. But increasingly we must wonder "What's God got to do with it?"—"it" being the faith that directs one's life.

The philosopher George Santayana insisted that no one can practice religion "in general." A living religion must be idiosyncratic and specific, that is, true to itself. It must press its claims to truth, and affirm obligations, some of which its adherents are bound to find onerous. A living religion is not simply a formula for an exclusive and affectionate relationship between creature and Creator, but a blueprint for personal obligation and social responsibility. In brief, religion is demanding. The scriptures of the major religions reveal that God deals with his creatures more corporately than individually, and that people have clear obligations to God and to one another—which explains churches, synagogues, and mosques—places where one may express corporate faith through worship as well as service to one's fellows.

In contrast, when one's mind is his church, God becomes each individual's benign prisoner, and each believer's responsibility is only to himself. Emerson long ago reduced religion to morality; today, particularly among the growing number of unchurched believers, religion has shrunk to sentiment and self-fulfillment.

That is not to suggest that Americans of all faiths are not generous or social-minded, but only that our religion is not communal, as in the past, but personal. As secular humanist Harold Bloom notes, we have revised traditional religion "into a faith that better fits our national temperament, aspirations, and anxieties."[9]

Just as commuters prefer the solitude and freedom of driving their own automobiles to taking public transportation, Americans increasingly prefer private faiths. Although religious books account for half the sales of all books in the United States, reading is a solitary act, nurturing faith that need not be articulated or shared. The growing preference for private faith explains the proliferation of fringe cults and sects in America, and their eccentric prophets. Cult members profess to have knowledge of revelations not available to the ordinary churchgoer, so they feel superior in their cocoons of faith.

The danger here, as in New Age thinking, is that God becomes indistinguishable from one's deepest inner self, and one begins to indulge in benign self-worship. Clearly, a faith so private is inadequate to motivate a nation to act in concert to realize the American Dream for all its citizens. Rather, such faith separates us.

In the history of the Christian church, the first heresy to appear was Gnosticism, whose adherents claimed to possess wisdom denied to other believers, and to have an inside track on God's affection. Bloom calls Gnosticism a "mass phenomenon" in contemporary America. "There are tens of millions of Americans," he says, "whose obsessive idea of spiritual freedom violates the normative basis of historical Christianity, though they are incapable of realizing how little they share of what once was considered Christian doctrine."[10] In other words, we have exchanged substance for sentiment.

The Weakness of the Mainline Churches

Against Puritan totalitarianism, Emerson preached, "It is by yourself without ambassador that God speaks to you. . . . It is God in you that responds to God without. . . ."[11]

Such a faith is private, unanchored by Scripture, creed, and doctrine; incommunicable; sentimental, buttressed only by the latest personal revelation. It listens to no human voice and needs no church for its expression. With notable exceptions, this is the faith of our nation in the twenty-first century. Granted, God is not dead, as naysayers claimed in the 1960s; rather we have absorbed and domesticated him.

How did this come to pass?

With the notable exceptions of the evangelical and Catholic churches, traditional Christianity has become accustomed since the Enlightenment to accommodating the secular culture. Sometimes known as the Age of Reason, the Enlightenment began in the eighteenth century to interpret human existence in terms contrary to religion. In the words of the historian Crane Brinton, the basic idea of the Enlightenment was "the belief that all human beings can attain here on earth a state of perfection hitherto in the West thought to be possible only for Christians in a state of grace, and for them only after death."[12]

The rationalists aimed at more than releasing mankind from superstition. They meant to free him from belief in, and responsibility to, a demanding God. Thomas C. Reeves identifies the Enlightenment as a secular religion in which pride (for Christians the worst of the seven deadly sins) is transformed into humankind's principal virtue.[13]

Not for nothing did Martin Luther call reason "the devil's harlot."[14] For Christians, the self is not the answer but the problem. It must be denied and mastered by repentance, humility, and reliance on God. However, Enlightenment thinking glorifies the self, which prompted C. S. Lewis to note tongue in cheek that "while it lasts, the religion of worshiping oneself is the best."[15]

Happily, the United States profited from founding fathers who balanced both religious and Enlightenment thinking. In retrospect, they may have been too optimistic about human nature, but optimism suited the New World and motivated our forebears. At the same time, the founders believed in an ordered universe, and they inherited from the Pilgrims a sense of destiny for this land.

Still, the Enlightenment planted a seed in America that would grow into secular humanism, forcing the churches to choose whether to accommodate pride as a virtue or to resist it as a vice. On balance, judging from performance, pride has conquered humility hands down. In the mainline churches in the new millennium there is more talk of self-esteem than of human frailty, and practically no mention of responsibility and sin. Rabbi Harold Kushner wrote a best-selling book whose title asked *How Good Do We Have to Be?* In it he argued that feelings of guilt and inadequacy, not sin and pride, are our downfall.

Accommodation and Capitulation

The scientific theory of evolution has long since been converted by nonscientists into a secular religion as well. The immediate impact of Charles Darwin's research was to depict life as the plaything of random and accidental forces, with survival only for the fittest. In such a relentless, mindless, evolving universe, there was no need of God. Still, the Church of England accommodated the evolutionists by burying Darwin in Westminster Abbey.

Rationalists seized upon the scientific theory to embrace change and enrolled themselves to hasten it. Thus the optimism of the Enlightenment combined with the notion that nature operates independent of any creator. With or without God, nature could be manipulated to serve human interests. Hence our current faith in technology and our willingness to tinker with genetic engineering. Once God is removed or discredited, man can take his place. Moreover, because only the fittest are meant to survive in an evolutionary universe, it was no longer incumbent on believers to assist the weak.

The mainline churches reacted to these secular religions by accommodating their premises and sanitizing their conclusions. Optimism, they sensed, might provide the motivation for a "social gospel" focused on building God's kingdom on earth. Perhaps some sense of evolution might help the faithful to pursue change for the good. Only the Evangelicals and Catholics met the challenges of the secular religions head-on, and then not always with success. Fundamentalists defended traditional faith by appealing to the Bible, whereas the mainline Protestant churches sought simply to ignore secular challenges to religious faith. This left ordinary Christians clinging to their faith as to a life raft. Predictably, the suspicion that Christian doctrine was vulnerable to secular challenge prompted many faithful Christians to retreat to a religion of private experience. Perhaps a sentimental faith could be substituted for a reasonable one.

By the end of the twentieth century, accommodation had turned into capitulation. Traditionally, no one expected religious faith to be *proven* by reason, but most people still assumed that it was *reasonable* to believe in a creator, a moral order, and an afterlife. Today it is the rare clergyman or woman who can respond to secular challenges to faith. Clergy are no longer accustomed to arguing for the truth of what they believe. Indeed the seminaries do not train them to confront the challenges and to defend the faith by reason. Instead, they rely on members to cling to religion for essentially emotional reasons.

The decline of dogma can be traced to the churches' lack of confidence in articulating why it is still sensible to believe. As a consequence, mainline clergy tend to minister exclusively to the spirits rather than to the minds of their members—a recipe for disaster.

Faith organizations exist to sustain and nourish what we possess in common—our beliefs. Our spiritual lives, by contrast, are idiosyncratic and can be pursued personally without reference to the church. When I joined the board of a consortium of twelve Protestant and Catholic theological schools, I scrutinized their combined course offerings to discover whether this challenge is being addressed in seminary training.

In brief, it is not. Within their combined curricula there is no course devoted to apologetics—the defense of faith against unbelief, affirming the reasonableness of religion. Yes, there is one course that attempts dialogue between science and religion, and another that seeks conversation between faith and secular philosophy, but that is it. Moreover, there are no more G. K. Chestertons, C. S. Lewises, or Frank Sheeds writing popular books today that provide reasons for believing. As a consequence, when my own adult daughters drifted from belief to doubt, I began writing letters to them about the faith in which they were raised, appealing to their minds as well as their hearts. When those letters were collected in a book, I titled it *Be Strong and Courageous*.[16]

Confident Faith

Faith is not an option but a necessity, because we act according to what we believe. William Murchison observes that "As morality is the heart of culture, so religion is the heart of morality,"[17] and good behavior is not contrived but learned. Churches not only offer the opportunity for worship but for loving service, which is at the heart of morality.

One would assume that the churches would support confident belief, but in mainline Protestantism at the moment, confidence is declining, and churchgoing is the residual habit of an aging population whose children have dropped out altogether. As early as 1983, close to half of all mainline churchgoers were fifty years of age or older.[18] With the decline of dogma, the churches have lost a sense of what makes them distinctive. The Reverend Jim Andrews, former head of the Presbyterian Church (USA), acknowledges that "churches without any self-understanding lose members."[19]

As members drift in uncertainty, church leaders hotly embrace controversy on peripheral issues. At the

Episcopal church's General Convention in 1994, for example, the House of Bishops wearied of dealing with the issue of gay ordination and left it to each prelate to do what he or she chose. Two observers concluded that "the Episcopal church is an institution in free fall. We have nothing to hold on to, no shared belief, no common assumptions, no agreed bottom line, no accepted definition of what an Episcopalian is or believes."[20]

Such intramural bickering distracts from the need for Americans of faith to apply their beliefs to realizing the American Dream for all. Exit polls in the 1994 election year revealed that a majority of Americans believed the nation's problems were not economic but "primarily moral and social."[21]

One would expect the churches to be in the front rank, confronting crime, violence, drug use, pornography, divorce, illegitimate births, child poverty, hunger, homelessness, inadequate medical care, and teen suicide, as well as plummeting standards in the nation's schools. Instead, distracted and with self-assurance in short supply, they lack solidarity. Ironically, while the mainline churches rally to provide aid to those suffering tragedies in other nations, they stumble with uncertainty here at home. Methodist theologian Stanley Hauerwas of Duke Divinity School claims that "God is killing mainline Protestantism in America, and we goddamn well deserve it."[22]

A Gallup poll reveals that only 27 percent of Protestants give their church an excellent rating. Evangelism and missionary work have suffered. As long ago as 1985, one-third of the nation's Methodist churches recorded no baptisms, and nearly two-thirds offered no new-member or confirmation classes.[23]

The Clergy's Confusion

David Carlson of the Evangelical Lutheran Church in America believes that the mainline churches have been co-opted by the secular culture, and blames their adherents' ignorance of Scripture, theology, and history. "We've lost the doctrinal underpinnings" of faith and practice, he says.[24] Some of the blame must rest with the clergy. Of the current generation of ministers issuing from mainline seminaries, Reeves comments, "Graduates often emerge with little faith in the integrity of Scripture, a minimal grasp of church history and orthodox theology, and armloads of politically correct positions on social and political issues."[25]

Dean Frederica Harris Thompsett acknowledges that the emphasis today at Episcopal Divinity School in Cambridge, Massachusetts, is feminine liberation theology—not the substance of the gospel.[26] Across town at Harvard University's Divinity School, a student admits, "Pluralism is the God at Harvard. The basic presumption is that Western religion is not good, and Christianity is the worst. The new slur, like being 'homophobic,' is being 'Christo-centric.'"[27] At Virginia's Episcopal Seminary, New Testament professor Katherine Grieb laments that not only is biblical literacy absent in her students, but "we're having to teach [them] English as well as teaching our disciplines."[28]

Reeves notes that, since the 1960s, seminaries have tailored their career preparation for ministry to the "felt needs" of their students, prompting "a decline in academic rigor and an emphasis on the therapeutic [and] the trendy." At Harvard Divinity School, students "who had not read an assignment could derail class discussion completely simply by accusing the author of sexism, homophobism, misogyny, or some similar offense."[29]

Reeves quotes Yale University Divinity professor Christopher R. Seitz's complaints about his students: "Most don't know the names of half of the books of the Bible, whether Calvin lived before or after Augustine, what it means to say that Christ descended to the dead or acted 'in accordance with the Scriptures,' what the wrath of God means, or how to understand a final judgment of the quick and the dead."[30]

Many mainline seminaries are producing clergy and lay leaders who align the church with the prevailing secular culture, uncritically crusading for feminism, abortion rights, and gay marriage and ordination. Increasingly, active homosexual and heterosexual seminarians move on to ordination even if they are not in monogamous relationships. In 1993, the draft statement on human sexuality issued by the Evangelical Lutheran Church in America caused an uproar in the denomination. Some read the document as providing the biblical justification for homosexuality and masturbation, and suggesting that teaching adolescents to use condoms was a moral imperative.[31]

Whether the mainline Protestant churches are right or wrong in these matters, their obsession with sexuality is a distraction from their responsibility to teach, minister, and serve. People of faith seek reasoned confidence, not controversy. Many of them, confused and underserved, retain formal church membership but become dropouts in practice. Their minds and hearts *become* their church not on principle but by default. Meanwhile, millions of unchurched Americans are ill-served by denominations that look inward. The churches cannot expect converts to their confusion.

The Religious Right

Reacting to the political correctness and the spiritual emptiness of the mainline churches, many fundamentalist Christians now not only defend dogma but attack the secular society. Although fewer than one in five Americans claims membership in the Religious Right, it remains a power within the Republican party, pressing a political agenda it believes squares with traditional religious values. Christian Rightists have a clear, if sometimes nostalgic, vision of the American Dream and a determination to redeem it.

The Religious Right famously favors an end to abortion on demand, opposes pornography and homosexual practice, and promotes prayer in the nation's public schools. It seeks to strengthen the marriage bond and preaches "family values." It blames moral slippage in America partly on the unwillingness of the mainline churches to stand up for their Christian convictions.

Many within the conservative movement acknowledge that morality cannot be legislated, but insist nonetheless that standards can be set and values can be nurtured in public and private life. They believe that a great nation founded on faith is disintegrating because political leaders tolerate irresponsible behavior under the guise of "compassion."

Religious Rightists are most credible when they focus on defending the family as the basic unit of society. Churches have always relied on families to nurture religious faith in their children, and society has never found a substitute for the family unit.

But restoring the traditional family may already be a lost cause. When we say "family," we think "children," and we assume marriage. In America that is no longer the case. Today, barely half of the nation's children live with both of their natural parents. Sociologist Tom Smith of the University of Chicago reports that "marriage has declined as the central institution under which households are organized and children are raised."

According to the National Opinion Research Center, the most common living arrangement today is a household of unmarried people with no children. Fully 62 percent of American households have no children at home.

What became of the traditional family that nurtured a churchgoing nation? It has suffered from a divorce rate that has doubled since 1960, plus a more than six-fold increase in the percentage of births to unmarried mothers. Women born after 1963 are ten times more likely to cohabit without benefit of clergy than women born thirty years earlier.

The Christian Coalition is the best-known organization representing the interests of the Religious Right. Its former executive director, Ralph Reed, claimed credit for the Republican sweep of Congress in 1994. "We're hot because we believe in something," he said then.[32] But Reed moved on, and the Coalition is increasingly skeptical about its ability to return the society to traditional values through legislation. Today it leans more toward teaching values through the family and through voluntary associations. Potentially, of course, the most powerful voluntary associations are church, synagogue, and mosque.

Faith Lost or Only Misplaced?

Arguably, in recent decades we have been so busy pursuing the American Dream of the good life for ourselves individually that we have neglected to nurture the faith on which that Dream is founded. If so, our only fault is inattention. If at the millennium our common faith has faltered or has shriveled for lack of nourishment or has been supplanted by sentimentality, at least we have not succumbed to cynicism. Faith has not been lost, only misplaced. As a people, we can retrieve it together and become responsible once again to God and our fellow man.

Chapter 5

Civil
Faith
and
Secular
Culture

*"Give to Caesar what belongs to Caesar,
and to God what belongs to God!"*
—Mark 12:17

THERE IS A POPULARLY-HELD NOTION THAT OUR NATION'S
founders separated church and state in order to protect government from religious influence. That notion
is wildly incorrect: rather, the republic's architects
aimed at freeing faith from the power of politics. The
First Amendment affirms freedom of conscience and
enjoins the state from meddling in its citizens' exercise
of faith. In this respect, the Constitution echoes Jesus's

practical wisdom: "Give to Caesar what belongs to Caesar, and to God what belongs to God."

Nevertheless, politicians continue to profess pieties that pretend that a vote for Caesar is a vote for God. Many end their speeches to the citizenry with a consoling "God bless you." When the elder President George H. W. Bush proclaimed that "by the grace of God, America won the Cold War," he linked the blessings of peace with the righteousness of his administration. When his son, campaigning for his party's nomination for president, was asked to name his role model, George W. Bush replied: "Jesus Christ, because he changed my heart." God, predictably, kept silent, while politicians of both parties aspired to be his spokesman.

Although there is a public faith that undergirds the American Dream, there is no national church. If there were, you can rest assured that it would be manipulated by the government. As it is, politicians seek the opportunity to preach pieties from any available pulpit. They appeal directly to our public faith to support their own vision of the American Dream. But as Yale's Stephen L. Carter warns, "Having lots of public religion is not the same as taking religion seriously."[1]

Another Republican candidate, Gary Bauer, taking his faith seriously, spelled out its consequences, quoting Jesus:

> I was hungry and you gave me food. I was thirsty and you gave me a drink. I was lonely and you made me welcome. I was naked and you clothed me. I was ill and you came and looked after me. I was in prison and you came to see me there (Matthew 25:35-36).

A public faith based on religion cannot translate into the American Dream unless it starts with a commitment to others.

The First Amendment, incidentally, prevents only the *federal* government from favoring one religious faith over others. The Constitution did not prohibit the states from doing so. Some states had legally-established churches until well into the nineteenth century and taxed their citizens to support them.

Today, ironically, the separation of church and state is interpreted in ways that prevent the public expression of faith by schoolchildren, but leave politicians free to preach pieties anywhere. Arguably, the "separation" clause cripples the ability of faith-based organizations to contribute all they can to the common weal. In many ways, religious organizations, unconstrained by bureaucratic red tape and funded by donations, serve public needs more effectively than government. And privately supported, faith-related classrooms, with only a fraction of the resources of the public schools, often serve their students better.

Moreover, while Congress debates about foreign aid in terms of the national interest, faith-sponsored organizations react instantly to humanitarian needs around the world, and remain there long after the journalists and politicians have lost interest. In Kosovo, for example, Christian and Jewish relief organizations were caring for Muslim refugees before the U.S. government took an interest, and they are still there. Incidentally, they did not distribute Bibles to the Muslims.

Humanitarianism and compassion are seldom merely secular virtues. Rather, they are animated by religious faith and by the impulse to share the

American Dream. In matters of chronic need—homelessness, health, poverty, education, employment, and peace—people of faith continue to prod a hesitant government to serve the common good.

The Elusiveness of Utopia

Americans survived a century of social engineering. Fortunately, in the twentieth century, fascism and communism failed, and wholesale socialism was tempered by privatization. In every instance around the world where government assumed godlike powers, human nature prevailed against dictatorship, and the state failed to be worthy of worship.

In the United States, we have largely avoided the inclination of government to dictate to both spirit and body. To be sure, the common weal rests not on government policy alone, but on a people who have faith in God and a commitment to one another. What Chesterton said about his faith can also be applied to the Dream: Christianity has not been tried and found wanting. It has been found difficult and has yet to be tried.

You will recall that the occasion for Jesus's remark about rendering to God and government what each deserves was his examination of a Roman coin. The denarius Jesus held bore the profiles of Tiberius and his mother, depicted as god and goddess. Jesus firmly but politely dismissed Caesar's divine presumption. Clearly, God and government each have a claim on us, but those claims are distinct. St. Paul made clear that taxes must be paid and just laws obeyed, but only God is to be worshiped. The problem of church and state is to honor their legitimate claims while preventing their encroachment on each other. If anything, that problem is aggravated when faith is fuzzy and religious observance is in decline.

History illustrates government's temptation to extend its power beyond the preservation of public order and assurance of justice. The state assumes moral stances, and dresses its pragmatic policies in the cloak of religious idealism. As Charles Colson suggests, the reason is twofold: "The state needs religious legitimization for its policies, and an independent church is the one structure that rivals the state's claim for ultimate allegiance."[2] Communism failed in Poland, notably, because religious conscience would not yield to the state's claims.

In the United States, the Christian Coalition is merely the best-known group that seeks to use the government to bring about a society it feels best represents the dictates of religious faith. Another activist organization, People for the American Way, has a blueprint for the American Dream that is marked by strong values but is not faith related. But all such groups lobby the government under the illusion that government ("Caesar") can be the instrument for creating the kingdom of heaven on earth.

That Jesus utterly rejected political power for himself and his followers argues that God has means other than politics to usher in the kingdom. Recall that, after Rome's fall, the church of Christ succumbed to the very temptation of temporal power that Jesus personally refused. Among the consequences were the failed Crusades and the dread Inquisition.

In the twentieth century, the Social Gospel movement seduced the churches into waging a crusade to eliminate social injustice through government legislation, choosing a worthy end but the wrong vehicle. The church assumed a political mission.[3] Ironically, that crusade is welcomed by many in the government. For example, candidates in the 2000 presidential campaign proposed employing "faith-based organizations" (a euphemism for the churches) to carry out Washington's social policy. And why not? By co-opting religiously-motivated volunteers and private contributions, government would save money. Regardless of political party, government welcomes a religious excuse to do what it wants to do anyway.

The Role of Religion in Public Life

The motto of the state of Ohio, "With God all things are possible," is a public expression of faith adopted, not two centuries ago, but in 1959. It was recently struck down by a federal court. However, at least five other states boast similar expressions of public faith. Our national motto, "In God we trust," also reflects contemporary belief. It was adopted in 1956, just two years after the phrase "under God" was added to the Pledge of Allegiance. Forget references to Founding Fathers in wigs and waistcoats and their views on religion. These are *modern* expressions of government's reliance on something more than the power of politicians and voters.

There are civic virtues as well as religious virtues, to be sure, but—like manners—they are only pragmatic. The lasting values that exemplify and drive a society derive their power from something more than a mere show of hands. Laws reflect moral presuppositions—prohibiting, allowing, or promoting certain behaviors based on a sense of right and wrong. In America, even as faith erodes, a consensus still exists that the origin of all values is God himself, and that individual conscience must grapple with public duty.

When Americans of good will disagree on public issues such as abortion, euthanasia, homosexuality, and pornography, they dispute not about what is practical and convenient, but about what is *moral*. As a consequence, religion, which bears a repository of values from generation to generation, cannot shrink to the sidelines, but must witness its wisdom publicly. The church, the synagogue, and the mosque are responsible for demanding that public life be moral. That does not require entering the political arena, of course, but it casts the church in the role of loyal critic of the state.

Still, the church cannot assume it has all the answers. It is on surer ground when it appeals to individual consciences, and much less certain when it preaches to nations. When she was asked by a visiting African chief to reveal the formula for her successful sixty-seven-year reign over the British Empire, Queen Victoria presented him with a Bible, declaring, "Here is the secret!"

Unfortunately, not even Jimmy Carter, our most overtly religious president, could claim that the Bible provides a clear blueprint for public policy. Indeed, the great churchman Martin Luther long ago argued that it is impossible "to rule a country, let alone the entire world, by the gospel." Luther explained that "God has placed human civil life under the dominion of natural reason, which has the ability to rule physical things," and concluded: "We need not look to scripture for advice."[4] So both church and state must be reasonable and must know their places.

Conflicting Values

Nowhere is there greater confusion between church and state today than in the matters of life and death. What, for example, is the moral issue involved in abortion? Liberal politicians typically consider abortion a tragedy, but not murder. They hold that the overriding value the state must protect is a woman's dominion over her body and her right to choose whether to give birth or to curtail a pregnancy.

Religion takes a much dimmer view of the right to end a potential human life, but polls indicate that many believers would reluctantly accede to abortion rights in cases of rape and danger to the mother's life. Accordingly, the churches, which know that only God gives life, have been unable to form a united front to lobby either for or against the practice.

If a citizen's freedom to choose continues to be the overriding value protected by government, then mercy killing as well will eventually be sanctioned despite complaints from the churches that euthanasia is only another name for suicide. Here, as with abortion, compassion tends to compromise the prohibition against taking life, including one's own. Nor do the churches speak with one voice about the morality of destroying human embryos in an attempt to improve the health of Americans with dread diseases or disabilities.

Politicians seldom lead public opinion; typically, they follow it. Hence the proliferation of polls alerting Washington, D.C., to the mood of the citizenry. When religious Americans waver on moral issues of a public nature, politicians will follow the path of least resistance. This is yet another consequence of popular faith that is a mile wide but only an inch deep. As a people, we value fairness. So, for example, many a Christian who would never consent to an abortion herself feels uneasy about imposing her values on another woman who does not share her religious beliefs. On critical issues of life or death, the churches have lost the conviction that each individual belongs not to himself or herself, but to God, and that it is God alone who gives life and can legitimately withdraw it. Almost alone among faith-based institutions, the Catholic church persists in pressing this principle without exceptions. That explains why the Catholic hierarchy continues to oppose contraception even when polls indicate that individual Catholics employ birth control as commonly as the general population.

It also explains why the Catholic church opposes capital punishment. By its reasoning, the criminal's life, no less than his victim's, belongs to God. Accordingly, the state cannot play God. But, of course, it does.

We can write laws that protect the public against criminal acts, but we can't legislate morality. Short of law, however, we can set standards of acceptable personal behavior, just as parents do for their children. It is the churches' inconsistency in applying life-and-death standards to private life that makes it difficult for them to promote standards for *public* life. As Americans recede from religious faith and observance, our national consensus on these issues dissolves.

Marriage and Other Matters

Until recently, for example, both religious and secular Americans agreed on the purpose of marriage. Marriage, after all, was a secular institution long before the great religions made their appearance in history to bless it. The wedded state did not require romance as an ingredient, but it did provide for exclusive sexual rights, the possibility of procreation, and mutual responsibility. Because the family is the cornerstone of society, the state has always taken an interest in marriage. Religion, in turn, blesses marriage as an institution because it provides the Creator with the human means of giving, nurturing, and protecting life. Christianity even adds a note of romance, hallowing marriage as a reflection of God's love for his church.

Today in America the very definition of marriage is in question, if not in shambles. Half of all marriages now end in divorce, so the wedded state has lost its primal quality of permanence. Moreover, sexual relations are widely indulged outside of marriage without mutual responsibility or fear of pregnancy. Childless cohabitation is more common than marriage. Today, two-thirds of all American households consist of adults only. Tragically, when babies do arrive, one in three are born to single mothers.[5]

This situation led the Vermont Supreme Court late in 1999 to grant the same rights to gay and lesbian couples as to wedded men and women, opening the way for same-sex marriage. The court's rationale was that of simple fairness. The inability of gay couples to conceive children was beside the point, the justices ruled, since many traditional couples choose not to have offspring, and indeed many long-term gay and lesbian households *do* include children, whether from previous marriages, artificial insemination, or adoption. The American Psychological Association reports that "home environments provided by gay and lesbian parents are as likely as those provided by heterosexual parents to support children's psychological growth."[6] Proponents of same-sex marriage argue that these children would benefit if their parents could marry and be adopted by the non-biological parents.

The state can do little to fix broken social institutions such as the family. They must be mended by the citizens who enjoy those institutions. Many denominations are hard-pressed to rationalize excluding gays and lesbians from their fellowship simply because they disapprove of their sexual predilections. If the churches hold out against gay wedlock by relying on homophobia alone, they will neither strengthen existing marriages nor promote marriage as a blessed state. Here is an instance in which the churches must rescue a social institution without recourse to the state. They must do it through setting standards for their own membership. But with faith in decline and believers setting their own standards, it is less likely than ever that the churches will succeed.

In the nineteenth century, slavery was outlawed largely because the churches agreed that it was a public sin. People of faith threw their moral weight against bondage. Lamentably, the civil rights movement of the 1960s was the last time the churches achieved a similar consensus. That movement was epitomized by its leader, a clergyman, Dr. King. Its righteousness persuaded the public, and the government followed suit. The civil rights crusade was a triumph for the churches, and they wisely did not take credit for its success, but proclaimed it a victory for all Americans.

In the twenty-first century, the churches are aware of the moral issues that impede the full realization of a just and generous society, but they lack consensus and conviction. Beset by their own problems, they turn inward. American justice and welfare both need reforming, but as yet the churches have reached no consensus on hunger, the plight of the homeless, or capital punishment.

Meanwhile, millions have no shelter and children have become our poorest citizens. Two million Americans languish in prison, and nearly another three million await trial or are on parole or in halfway houses. Scores are executed each year. Ironically, although most crimes are victimless, few victims of crime are compensated for what they have lost. Because the churches do not know what to tell government to do, they have only a small voice in justice.[7]

Education

There is, however, a growing consensus among the churches that separation of church and state is unwittingly promoting secularism, turning public institutions into environments hostile to religion. Nowhere is the exclusion of faith's expression more resented than in the nation's public schools. In heavily Christian communities, especially in the South, officials permit and even encourage school-sponsored prayers, despite federal court bans. In Celina, Texas, for example, prayers were still recited over the public address system before high school football games even after a prohibition by a U.S. Court of

Appeals. Is anyone really injured by such public professions of faith?

The Willis family of Troy, Alabama, answers yes. When the couple moved from Seattle to Troy in 1991, their three children became the only Jews in the Pike County public schools. They were forced to participate in Christian prayers and events. Eleven-year-old Sarah was told by a preacher invited by school officials that students would go to hell if they did not accept Jesus.

Her older brother had his head forced down by a teacher when fellow students bowed in prayer at school assemblies. Paul, the eldest, was required to write an essay titled "Why God Loves Me" as a form of discipline. A teacher told the Willis children, "If parents will not save souls, we have to."

The American Civil Liberties Union took the Willises' case and, in 1999, the county was enjoined from promoting religion in its schools and required to protect students from religious harassment. It was also required to allow students to exercise their faith and display its various symbols. The school officials had formerly refused to allow David, the middle child, to wear a star of David lapel pin in the classroom.

The Willis case is an extreme example, but such cases force both church and state to delineate their roles in American society. Within the last several years new federal guidelines have affirmed that the state cannot impose religion in the schools, nor can students be forced to be secular against their will.

It is a delicate distinction, but common sense nonetheless. Individual students may pray if they wish. Jewish students may wear skullcaps, and Muslim girls may wear head scarves. Students may talk about religion and keep Bibles on their desks. The government also urges that religious minorities be accommodated insofar as possible in observing their holy days. The working principle is that religious freedom requires the government to keep out of the way at the same time it protects free expression of faith. As President Clinton explained before he left office, the Constitution "does not require children to leave their religion at the schoolhouse door."[8]

As for the continued ban on organized prayer in the public schools, even so committed an evangelical Christian as Charles Colson supports it. He argues that

Children or teachers who want to pray in schools should have the same rights of free expression and the same access to public facilities any other group has. But organized prayer, even if voluntary, is another matter. The issue is who does the organizing? If it is the school board, Caesar is being given a spiritual function; admittedly a small crack in the door, but a crack nonetheless. I for one don't want my grandchildren reciting prayers determined by government officials. And in actual practice they would be so watered down as to be of no effect except perhaps to water down my grandchildren's growing faith.[9]

A consensus is growing among the churches (and supported by the courts) that it is in the interests of poor students underserved by their public schools to be able to attend private schools at public expense. Affordable private schools are typically church-sponsored. It is a legitimate concern of the state that children of other faiths (or no faith at all) be protected from proselytism in church schools. But it is not the state's right to demand that these schools expound only secular values. Milwaukee's Oklahoma Avenue Lutheran School tells prospective parents, "If you don't want your children to take part in our religion, our school's not for you. It's a Christian education. That's what we're about."

That's an extreme example. The Catholic St. Vincent Pallioto School is more typical. It tells parents of voucher students that if they keep insisting on keeping their children out of all religious activities, the youngsters may have to sit out in the hall.

In 1971 the U.S. Supreme Court ruled that public support of religious schools must not involve "excessive entanglement between church and state." Religious schools are perfectly willing to render to Caesar the things that are Caesar's, but they exist to render to God the things that are God's.

Private Faith, Public Values

Former presidential contender Bill Bradley faulted none of his rivals for "open expressions of their faith," but declared: "I've decided that personal faith is private, and I will not discuss it with the public." In that instance, it was probably a safe statement. George W. Bush, having earlier declared that Jesus "changed his heart," could not explain to the public what effect that change would have on him as president. "Well," Bush said, "if they don't know, it's going to be hard to explain."

Columnist E. J. Dionne Jr. reacted sensibly. "But it is surely a legitimate public issue if a candidate's religious convictions will affect the way he will govern. Isn't that something all of us should want to know?"[10]

Early in the 2000 presidential campaign, a group of one hundred Christian and Jewish leaders called for a moratorium on protestations of piety by political candidates. "We aren't looking for a convert or a congregant," said the Reverend Johnny Ray Youngblood. "We need a president who has the clarity and strength to tackle what we believe to be the core, corrosive issue of our time—the presence of a vast group of working poor in the midst of plenty."[11]

Religious faith is not simply personal, emotional, and habitual, but practical. To merely proclaim that I love my wife does not fulfill my part of the marriage contract. Marriage, no less than religion, is about faith. It is for richer and poorer, in sickness and in health, until death do us part. It's about responsibility and trust. For that matter, it's about routines like having meals on the table and taking out the trash. J. Bryan Hehir of Harvard Divinity School acknowledges that "religion is certainly about the heart, but it's about more than the heart. It's about an intellectual structure of belief, and a candidate needs to explain what that intellectual structure is about."[12] Faith has both substance and repercussions that are public and can be explained. Unfortunately, the religious faith of most political leaders is as shallow and inarticulate as that of the typical believer.

Frederick Mark Gedicks defines the faith common to most Americans at the millennium as "faintly Protestant platitudes which reaffirm the religious base of American culture despite being largely void of theological significance."[13] Sociologist Robert Wuthnow suggests that the only theological significance of our political faith may be "America First."[14] Yale's Carter insists that we are comfortable with platitudes because they demand nothing of us. Not only are they easily ignored by those who happen to have no religious beliefs, but they make virtually no demands on the consciences of those who do. God is thanked for the success of an enterprise recently completed or asked to sanctify one not yet fully begun. God is asked to bless the nation, its people, and its leaders. But nobody . . . is asked to do anything for God.[15]

The acerbic critic Gore Vidal, an astute chronicler of American political history, rails at American politicians who routinely clothe themselves in the raiment of religion and pander platitudes to the faithful. Vidal lives much of the year in Italy, which he loves for being paganly "pre-Christian," and believes Northern Europe to be "post-Christian," long since having wearied of faith and emptied its churches.

Monotheism itself, Vidal claims, is to blame for America's self-absorption and self-righteousness, as well as for its politicians' predilection to regulate citizens' lives and to preach to other nations. Our leaders demonize our international enemies, while fining, imprisoning, and executing those fellow citizens who deviate from righteousness. Political correctness is, in Vidal's view, only the latest expression of the religious righteousness assumed by the American state.[16]

State vs. Church

Occasionally, political righteousness in America is directed against the free expression of religion itself. The most notorious case in recent memory was the government's siege of the Branch Davidian community,

Mount Carmel, in Waco, Texas, in 1993. After a fifty-one-day standoff in which the community's members were effectively imprisoned and starved within the compound's walls, government agents stormed the site. In the ensuing conflagration seventy-five men, women, and children died from fire and suffocation.

Although we still claim to be a religious nation, Americans tend to be annoyed by sects that proselytize, and alarmed by cults that are exclusive and secretive. So, when government agents first surrounded the Branch Davidian compound, there was no public outcry, and the churches kept silent about the government's breach of the wall between church and state. At the time many of us, I suspect, sympathized with a reporter on the scene, who reflected, "There's no nut like a religious nut."

Agreed, the Branch Davidians were anything but typical Christians. They bore all the marks of a cult: exclusive, elitist, apocalyptic, led by a fanatical messiah who controlled their financial assets and their lives. But Waco survivor Clive Doyle asks of the government, "If they thought we were a bunch of crazies, why did they drive us to the limit?"[17] Federal agents insisted that the cult members set the fire themselves, but another survivor, David Thibodeau, dismisses that explanation. "If we really wanted to kill ourselves," he says, "we would not have waited fifty-one cold, hungry, scary days to do it."[18]

Ironically, federal officials besieging the compound only confirmed what David Koresh, the cult's leader, was telling his followers—that the world would end in a conflagration, pitting the forces of evil against a faithful remnant. As many as seven hundred armed insurgents trapped the cult members in their compound without supplies. Impatient, they finally appealed to Washington for permission to storm Mount Carmel with armored vehicles and tear gas, persuading the attorney general that Koresh was molesting minors among his disciples.

In fact, the self-styled "sinful messiah" had been having sex with young members all along, with the complicity of the girls' parents. But he forced no one to stay with him. Indeed twenty older members left freely when the siege began, leaving the faithful remnant to remain to their deaths. The irony is that Koresh could have been seized easily by officials before the siege.

In 1999 it was revealed that the FBI covered up its use of incendiary ammunition that could have caused the Waco fire, prompting the attorney general to authorize an independent investigation. To lead the inquiry she chose former Republican Senator John Danforth. Revealingly, he is also the *Reverend* Danforth, an active Episcopal priest, who took both law and divinity degrees at Yale. Given that wrinkle, it was ensured that Danforth would look not only at individual culpability in the Waco tragedy, but at the government's intrusion into the exercise of religious freedom at Waco.

Individual government agents were subsequently cleared of negligence at trial and in the Danforth Report, but the violence and devastation of the Waco siege continues to worry those who believe that the state bullies faiths it does not favor.

History confirms that the government has nothing to fear, and everything to gain, from a faithful citizenry. Although the churches seldom speak with a single voice on public issues, they cannot be expected to remain silent when government presumes to breach the separation of church and state.

America, while blessed, is not yet the kingdom of God on earth. Caesar is Caesar, and God is God. The ultimate loyalty of church, temple, and mosque will always transcend the nation. People of faith will be concerned not only with the American Dream for themselves and their children, but with the common good of all human beings everywhere. Ultimately we are responsible to—and we answer to—a transcendent God who holds the whole world in his hands.

Chapter 6

Redeeming
the
American
Dream

God, not man, is the final authority.
God has rights. Human beings have duties;
we deny God his rights at our peril.
—Paul Johnson

DR. MARTIN LUTHER KING JR. EVOKED THE AMERICAN Dream of a just and generous society in his first major civil rights sermon in Montgomery, Alabama, declaring, "If we are wrong, Jesus of Nazareth was merely a utopian dreamer and never came down to earth! If we are wrong, justice is a lie!"[1] More than three decades after Dr. King's assassination, the Dream still eludes many Americans.

With faith in decline, fewer Americans are persuaded that it is neither utopian nor a lie.

In the State of the Union message each January, our nation's presidents trumpet the accomplishments of their administrations, as if the perennial Dream is on the verge of being realized. But what is the actual state of the union early in the third millennium, and what can Americans do to perpetuate the Dream in a nation that is losing its faith?

The novelist and critic John Updike attempted an early assessment of the quality of life in America when he answered a *Forbes* magazine question: "Why, when Americans have it so good, do we feel so bad?" He answered, "The question suggests its own answer; because Americans *had* it so good, they feel bad now."[2] In many respects, Updike notes that the Dream has fragmented in recent years, and we are worse off than before.

I feel a kinship with Updike, not least because we were both born during the Great Depression, when expectations were low but appreciation was high, and life was safe. As the Depression babies grew to adulthood, our quality of life improved, until we reached parenthood and discovered that the world in which our own children live is neither safe nor affordable. My wife and I both worked our way through private colleges and graduate schools, helped by scholarships and fellowships, and actually emerged with a few dollars left in our pockets to confront the world of work.

That is no longer possible. One of our daughters compiled college debts of $40,000 in the process of becoming qualified for social work, serving AIDS patients, the homeless, addicts, and poor immigrant parents and their young children. Rest assured, the good Samaritan of the gospel did not run up such debts in order to assist the needy of his day. All three of our daughters are older than thirty, yet only one of them as yet has been able to afford an apartment of her own. The escalating costs of education and housing have battered the American Dream.

The Old Get Rich and the Young Get Poorer

Not so long ago, the elderly were the poorest segment of the population. Now our poorest are the nation's children—one in five youngsters lives below the poverty line, is undernourished, poorly educated, and deprived of adequate health care. Thirty million Americans do not know where their next meal is coming from. Poverty in America, incidentally, is not confined to racial minorities in our cities. The majority of poor Americans are white and live outside the cities, where we cannot see them.

Meanwhile, families are broken. Police are hard-pressed to secure the domestic peace. In intact families, both spouses must work to make their way, leaving latchkey children to fend for themselves after school.

Updike is not being sentimental when he remembers public buildings that reflected the nation's pride in their architecture. Today, he notes, our "high schools no longer look like castles but like second-rate airports, low-slung and cut-rate." He, too, laments how unaffordable life has become for our children. "My generation," he reflects, "lived better than its parents, which made us feel good; but we live better than our children, which makes us feel bad."[3]

What adults of my generation experienced may not have been a golden age, but it was closer to the Dream for some of us then than for all of us now. In the new century we have exchanged necessities—affordable housing, education, and health care—for cell phones and computer games. Young adults, scraping by financially, now settle for "relationships" rather than marriage. The great majority of Americans have saved nothing toward retirement. Individually, we are a nation of debtors, maxed-out on our credit cards. Without our noticing, former luxuries have become more affordable than present necessities. Even the poor manage to afford color televisions, vacation packages, and $100 sneakers for their children. But housing, health care, college, and day care strain the budgets of the middle class. Before the War on Poverty in the 1960s, sociologist Michael Harrington remarked that America's poor were "invisible" to us, because they wear the same clothes as other Americans. But that was before our city sidewalks became populated by bag ladies and homeless men, sleeping on grates wrapped in newspaper against the cold.

Dr. King's dream for people of color is not even close to being realized in America. Racism reflects only one of the phobias we disguise with political correctness. Michael Jordan and Tiger Woods may be the heroes of white American teenagers, but racism runs deep among their elders. Black comedian Chris Rock was perceptive when he taunted a white audience: "There's not one of you would change places with me— and I'm a *millionaire!*"

The Role of Religion

It's a temptation to think of these as purely political problems. In fact, they are challenges to a declining faith in God and in one another. As a nation we may lack strictly "religious" solutions to societal problems, but faith is custodian of the values that define the American Dream and govern what people of good will expect from our society and are willing to give to it. It is easy to feel impotent to change the quality of our lives, and it is difficult to assign responsibility in our complex world. But difficulty is not impossibility.

For example, we breathed a collective sigh of relief when we entered the new millennium without the world's computer systems wreaking havoc on our lives by breaking down. The cost of Y2K "repairs" to those systems was estimated to be as high as one trillion dollars worldwide.

Lost in our euphoria is the fact that the problem was not only predictable but had been anticipated by software manufacturers forty years earlier. At slightly greater cost they could have made the world's computers recognize the year 2000, but they chose to build cheaper, more profitable products, ultimately passing the problem to the world's governments, corporations, and financial institutions to fix.

Ultimately one trillion dollars, which could have been invested in improving the quality of life around the world, was lost to repairing a predictably faulty product. The day after Y2K never happened, poor nations around the world expressed their outrage that they had been required to spend billions in borrowed dollars to fix a technological problem of someone else's making.

Morality cannot be legislated; nevertheless, all legislation reflects shared values. Religion exemplifies those values and can urge them on society at large. The Christian Coalition, having long pressed a political agenda with only modest success, now inclines to believe that values are best promoted in society *outside* government. That means within the family and religious, charitable, and educational institutions. If American society is to reclaim the American Dream, the Coalition's leaders reason, it will not be because Washington imposes laws, but because ordinary Americans live up to their beliefs and encourage their neighbors to do the same. The idea is to rebuild our society from the bottom up, rather than from the top down. But as faith declines, our resolve weakens.

The unwillingness of the churches to affirm standards renders them largely impotent to attract unchurched people and help to redeem the American Dream. Today compassion is too often only another word for sentimentality. When President Bill Clinton revealed that he "feels our pain," he meant only that he felt sympathy for us. By contrast, when Jesus took compassion on sinners and the sick, he insisted that they have a change of heart with a consequent change in behavior. Today the churches are judgmental about internal, parochial problems, like gay and female ministry, but they have largely abandoned their prophetic role to appeal to the consciences of society at large. That abandonment is reflected in the decline of missionary movements within our mainline denominations. Fearful of being accused of proselytism, we increasingly hoard the riches of our faith for ourselves. But those riches are less and less esteemed as Americans fall away from the practice of faith.

The Social Gospel

Because spirituality today is perceived in such personal terms, people of faith tend to focus on the first part of the Great Commandment—to love the Lord God—and less on the second part—to love one's neighbor. As Americans cherish feeling over action and intimacy over service, their churches neglect to correct them. Today Protestants and Catholics alike agree that it is faith that saves, not works. But faith has consequences, including responsibilities to create a just and loving society. The only faith worth its name is a *working* faith. Not so long ago this was precisely what the churches attempted to inculcate, and with notable success.

Early in the twentieth century Christianity's sense of stewardship reached its apogee in the Social Gospel movement. After centuries of disputation, liberal Protestantism tired of speculation and the search for individual perfection, and turned instead to crafting heaven on earth. In retrospect, the Social Gospel movement appears naively utopian, but as late as 1961, half the students in major divinity schools called it the greatest achievement of the previous half-century.

It was a largely American enterprise, but it reflected the yearning of the English poet William Blake to establish a new Jerusalem in his own country:

I will not cease from mental fight,
Nor shall my sword sleep in my hand,
Till we have built Jerusalem
in England's green and pleasant land.[4]

Blake had railed against his own nation's "dark Satanic mills,"[5] but in America we had sweat shops and child labor as well. Life on earth was far from heavenly. Walter Rauschenbusch, an American theologian who died in 1918, insisted that the kingdom of God must be made real on earth by people of faith. Heaven, he preached, was not a reality to be encountered after death, but the symbol of a world to be made perfect now. He called for a return to the basic Gospel teachings that sought social justice in our present lives. Heaven can wait, he preached; the church's mission was to create the New Jerusalem here and now.

In the late nineteenth century, as believers increasingly focused on their personal pursuit of salvation, the churches lost interest in working with God to create a fair and just world. Hope, Rauschenbusch countered, must be for the present, not a future reality. His call was heeded. In Europe, between the two World Wars, Christian socialist parties pursued the Social Gospel. In the United States the churches, assisted by articulate theologians such as the Protestant Reinhold Niebuhr and the Catholic John Courtney Murray, called upon business, government, and the schools to liberate all Americans from misery and to seek equality of opportunity and treatment.[6]

Nationwide conditions of hardship during the Great Depression hastened legislation and regulation to that effect, and the New Deal was followed by the Fair Deal and the Great Society. The churches thought they knew what was needed, and they persuaded the nation to act in its common interests. The National Council of Churches was formed to present a united front. Not surprisingly, the churches not only supported the

League of Nations and the United Nations, but served these international organizations through their own service agencies.

Retreat from the Kingdom

Welfare agencies affiliated with the churches are still in the front line of service in times of disaster and need. The American Friends Service Committee, a Quaker organization, won the Nobel Peace Prize following World War II for relief work in Europe. Christian, Jewish, and Islamic service organizations, privately-funded, were in Kosovo assisting refugees long before governments became involved, and they remained to help in reconstruction. The pattern of assistance is repeated in areas of need worldwide.

But ever since the civil rights movement of the 1960s and the decline of faith, the American churches have largely lost their voice and their influence here at home. At the outbreak of the Persian Gulf War, the White House was picketed by no less a personage than the presiding bishop of the Episcopal Church, who condemned the conflict as bloodshed for mere oil rights. The elder President Bush, a prominent and faithful Episcopalian, brushed off the protest as mere political opinion. Over the years, the nation's Roman Catholic bishops have taken thoughtful, detailed positions on issues such as nuclear war, the economy, and homelessness, but they are treated by Washington, D.C., as just another pressure group with an axe to grind.

In recent years the most prominent clergyman speaking to the nation's social conscience was the Reverend Jesse Jackson, but he represents no church group. That may have been an advantage, because one need not bother to seek church consensus in order to speak out politically.

Jackson does not take the time to educate the consciences of church members, only to disturb them. That's understandable: there is only one of him. But *bona fide* church leaders do not go to the trouble of educating or consulting either. The presiding bishop of the Episcopal Church did not consult his faithful before taking a stand against the Persian Gulf War, nor did his clergy seek to persuade faithful Episcopalians afterwards. The Catholic bishops seek only their own consensus before taking positions on public issues. Rank-and-file Catholics are neither consulted nor educated. The National Council of Churches has taken consistently liberal positions on public policy since the 1960s without reference to the beliefs of ordinary American Christians and without informing them. Not surprisingly, its pronouncements are politely ignored by government.

Policymakers insulate themselves from church pressure by taking polls. They *know* what the citizenry is thinking—including the non-observant majority who still claim to be believers. By contrast, the churches are ignorant of what their members feel about public policy, and the pulpit is seldom devoted to controversial matters of conscience that reflect religious values. Accordingly, piety has scant chance of persuading policymakers.

Making an Impact

In early 2000 President Clinton invoked God in offering this millennial prayer for the nation:

Help us now to accept at long last the enduring truth that the most important fact of life is not wealth, or power, or beauty, or scientific advance, but our kinship as brothers and sisters, and our oneness as children of God.[7]

No ordained preacher could express the nation's public faith better than that. But it flies in the face of the facts.

As for wealth, the richest 1 percent of Americans own 39 percent of the nation's wealth. Even after taxes this 1 percent enjoys as much income as the one hundred million poorest-paid Americans *combined*. The poorest one-fifth of Americans actually earn 9 percent less in real terms that they did more than twenty years ago. Despite relatively low unemployment, recent college graduates are earning $2 per hour less than their counterparts did more than a decade ago, while high school graduates lost one-fourth their earning power in the same period.[8]

As for power, even the president could not deny its seductiveness. On the subject of beauty, Americans spend more for diets, cosmetics, and plastic surgery than they do on the poor. As for scientific advance, it is so precious to us that Washington, D.C., frightened the rest of the world into spending upward of one trillion dollars just to fix its computers.

Finally, as to our kinship as brothers and sisters, the most trumpeted accomplishment of the 1990s was to cut the nation's welfare rolls. It was what the people wanted: the unemployed poor were draining tax dollars from working Americans. In that event, one would expect the religious community to have been vocal advocates for the poor. But during the debates of welfare reform, the churches stood on the sidelines, and they have since neglected to inform their members of some of the dire consequences of reform on the lives of our neediest citizens.

Despite a potentially resilient economy, the condition of Americans who remain poor has actually worsened. Census data show they have dropped further below the poverty line. What remains of the safety net has weakened. Of families with children that remain poor, fewer are receiving either cash assistance or food stamps. Whereas welfare used to be the gateway to Medicaid, many families who are still legally eligible for subsidized health care no longer receive it. State coffers are filled with the savings. As the *Washington Post* editorialized:

> Welfare reform represented a shift of responsibility to the states. A weak federal guarantee of support for low-income families with children was replaced by none. The decline in the rolls has saved them large amounts of money; they are enjoying a welfare dividend.[9]

Of course, church-related agencies continue to serve Americans in need, but their efforts are distant from the awareness and involvement of most Americans who are still church-goers. Today the church has so separated itself from the state that it appears no longer capable of effectively pressing perennial values on the political process. Worse, it shrinks from reminding its members what those values are. No wonder a mile-wide faith is only a inch deep.

Advocacy Groups

Like voices crying in the wilderness, religious advocacy groups attempt to accomplish what the churches themselves have largely abandoned: bringing the remnants of religious faith and values to bear on defining and promoting the American Dream of a just and generous society.[10] Four hundred such groups existed at the end of World War II. They have since been joined by about five hundred more. In the past twenty years these "para-church" organizations have grown faster than the churches themselves. Most of the newer ones neither originated with denominations nor are sponsored by them. The best are interdenominational and self-funded, and operate on a shoestring.

Mel Reese is the director of the Ecumenical Alliance for Peace and Justice, one of the broadest-based groups. He laments the retreat of the churches from public life. "There is a sickness setting in now in the mainline churches," he believes. "It's as if people have lost a vision that stretches out over the society. So now they're turning inward and tearing at each other, 'reorganizing' instead of getting on with the public business at hand. We have a lot of internal factional politics—fratricidal politics, really. You build a strong activist organization, get things done, and denominational leaders are scared you're not 'bringing everyone along in the churches.'"[11]

Accordingly, Reese does not restrict his budget to subsidies from denominations, but looks to funding from local churches, dioceses, foundations, and unrelated individuals who seek social and economic justice. Among liberal and moderate Protestants, for example, there is broad support for environmentalism, nuclear disarmament, foreign aid, drug rehabilitation programs, child welfare, improved public education, and aid to the homeless. There is less consensus on other issues such as capital punishment, military spending, subsidized health care, abortion, and Affirmative Action.

Conservative advocacy groups have different agendas, but Reese says, "I'm not so worried about fighting it out with the evangelicals. I see a lot of them recognizing the positive role of the church in social action besides soup kitchens and shelters. They know about food stamps, too. They're for peace and civil rights."[12] But he and other advocates worry that most congregations are not only shrinking but myopic, focusing on internal concerns rather than the society at large. "Pulling back into the local church and prescribing 'community' for whatever ails us is giving up the hope that we really can make the whole society any more just or caring," Reese believes.[13] It means treating faith as a personal possession while giving up on the American Dream for all but those closest to us.

Something Less than Paradise

Religious advocates in Washington, D.C., lament the churches' faltering social mission, but they do not pretend that legislation alone will create the kingdom of God on earth. Reese says, "The church's social role is not to design a perfect society. It's to make the existing society *more* caring."[14] A narrow religious vision can only create a narrow society, so a truly ecumenical agenda is necessary. That requires collaboration as well as mission.

Reese and other advocates do not bide their time waiting for consensus among Christians before they act. Instead, they aim to educate both policymakers and the churches about real conditions in the society. "Our approach to particular issues is to try to ask where the justice of it lies, which position on it makes for a more just society," he says. "Justice means taking care of one another."[15]

For example, before the welfare reforms of the last decade, a group of ecumenical and denominational agencies sought to improve the government's Aid to Families with Dependent Children programs. To justify their political recommendations, they turned to a professor of Old Testament studies, who helped them define American society's responsibility for its children. Children, the theologian insisted, are nothing less than God's gift to a people who were once children themselves. Unless society cares for its children, it trespasses against the covenant with their Creator. Once armed with this sense of moral gravity, the recommendations began to be taken seriously by policymakers.

Some critics of advocacy groups believe that the churches should concentrate on direct voluntary action instead of seeking remedies from the government. But injustices within the society are too great to be solved by private and local efforts alone, even when the government supports faith-based initiatives. Homelessness and inadequate health care are too widespread to be met by volunteerism and private funding alone. Church-sponsored schools cannot compensate for tax-funded public schools that are failing the nation's children. Habitat for Humanity, for example, spends several hundred thousand dollars to build houses for no more than ten families, using free labor. "Spend that much to change HUD regulations, clean up

HUD, fund it adequately, and you could house five thousand or five million families," Reese argues. "You have to bring in the state."[16]

Robert Cooper leads one of the largest Methodist congregations in the urban South. He is evangelically inclined, but agrees with the more liberal Reese about creating a just society. Nevertheless, Cooper concentrates not on legislation, but on educating the consciences of his members to ensure that they possess both a spiritual and a social vision. "My main concern about the . . . mainline denominations," he says, "is not that they are in error or heresy, but that their priorities are wrong. We're straining at gnats and swallowing camels."

Cooper believes the churches must speak out on politics, because "Jesus is Lord of the whole of our lives," but acknowledges that reforming society will not "bring the Kingdom of God any closer." For Cooper, worship, ministry, and discipling are the building blocks of a just society. He seeks to form "apostles" who "put into practice Christ's word and love in their home, in their neighborhood, in their job and school." But with religiously-involved Americans now only a minority of the citizenry, there are fewer candidates for that mission.[17]

The Substance of the Dream

If religious faith is defined simply as a personal acknowledgment of God's existence, then there is no question that faith is still widespread in America. As a people, we may not fear God as our forebears did, but most of us still believe in him, and we seek his aid in our personal and domestic lives.

But personal faith has social consequences, and the whole is greater than the sum of its parts. The Great Commandment compels love and service to both God and neighbor. In this respect, the future of faith in America is tenuous. There is ample evidence that, for many, God is an afterthought, and the majority of Americans are failing one another in pursuing a just and generous society for all.

Some dismiss the American Dream as little more than the quest for material affluence. But even the most devout citizens are not pure spirits; they are flesh and blood, not angels. All of God's creatures need jobs and clothing, food and housing, health care and education, safety and security. Jesus cannot be accused of materialism because he fed the hungry, gave drink to the thirsty, healed the sick, showed mercy toward criminals, taught the ignorant, and comforted widows and orphans. Born homeless, sleeping out of doors with only a rock for a pillow, Jesus experienced hardship. In a poignant appeal, he taught that what we do to assist the least of his brethren, we do for him.

The American Dream falls far short of the kingdom of heaven on earth, but it is an expression of our lingering faith in God and one another. It must be redeemed. We can still be the shining city on the hill that the pilgrims sought to build. But there is much to be overcome before we achieve a just society. Former Secretary of Education William J. Bennett paints a picture that is closer to nightmare than Dream:

> The nation we live in today is more violent and vulgar, coarse and cynical, rude and remorseless, deviant and depressed, than the one we once inhabited. A

popular culture that is often brutal, gruesome, and enamored with death robs many children of their innocence. People kill other people, and themselves, more easily. Men and women abandon each other, and their children, more readily. Marriage and the American family are weaker, more unstable. . . .[18]

In recent decades the Dream has faded along with the religious faith that inspired it. Since the election of John F. Kennedy our population has increased by half. In the same period we have experienced nearly a five-fold increase in violent crime, in Americans behind bars, and in out-of-wedlock births. Today there are three times as many children living in single-parent homes, and ten times as many couples choosing to cohabit without the security and commitment of marriage. Meanwhile the nation's divorce rate has doubled.

In a nation of mile-wide, inch-deep faith, life is treated cheaply. In the past quarter-century there have been close to forty million abortions. Between 1970 and 1996 the percentage of American children living in poverty increased by one-third. We continue to execute fellow Americans despite no evidence that capital punishment is a deterrent to crime and despite evidence that many on death row are innocent. Since the U.S. Supreme Court reinstated capital punishment, scores of men and women under sentence of death have been freed on DNA testing alone.

Redeeming the Dream
The pilgrims saw America as a shining example to the world of the power of faith to redeem individuals and create a caring society. But today, as faith weakens, the

United States leads the developed world in divorce, single-parent families, abortion, sexually transmitted diseases, child poverty, incarceration, and executions, as well as drug use and out-of-wedlock births among teens. We deny health care to a larger percentage of citizens than any other developed nation. Although we spend more on the education of our children than any nation except Austria and Switzerland, by the time they graduate from high school their math and science skills are worse than other developed nations.

Some of these shameful statistics reflect a decline in personal morality, which in turn reflects the waning of religious faith. Others can be remedied by public policy if affluent Americans are willing to share the Dream with those less fortunate. But in every case the church, the synagogue, and the mosque can be effective in appealing to hearts, minds, and consciences. We do not need a revival of faith that is other-worldly. *This* is God's world now. As we share its space with one another, we must share its bounty and its justice.

In the very darkest ages of faith, there was an institution that welcomed the homeless, the sick, the hungry, and the frightened. It gave protection to widows, education to children, and sanctuary to those who repented of crimes. That institution was the cloister. There were many monasteries scattered around Christendom, havens from a Roman Empire that could no longer protect its citizenry. These self-sufficient communities are prized today for having protected the art and literature of ancient civilizations. But in their time they were more: they were the most civilized places on earth. They dispensed humanity, and they did so because they were motivated by religious faith.

Today in America our institutions—education, health care, affordable housing, secure employment, marriage, and family among them—are in free-fall. We have shut the doors of our mental health facilities, schools for orphans, settlement houses, and institutions for troubled youth, and cut back on public housing. Is it any wonder that the poor, the homeless, the mentally ill, and the alienated roam our streets? The only public institution enjoying healthy growth in America is prison construction.

The Future of Faith

The final year of the second Christian millennium produced an unlikely American martyr, a seventeen-year-old girl at Columbine High School in Colorado. Held at gunpoint, Cassie Bernall was asked by a fellow student whether she believed in God. She answered yes. Before she could answer his next question —why?—he killed her. We will never know whether Cassie could have saved her life by denying her faith. What we do know is that she spoke the truth despite the consequences.

To redeem the American Dream, we need not be martyrs to our faith, but we must be true to it, deepen it, and accept its consequences. If faith has a future in America, it cannot simply consist of a serene inner life. Faith must motivate action. As Paul Johnson reminds us: God has rights, we have duties. Faith alone, he acknowledges, "cannot end war, cruelty, greed, and the miseries of the poor. But it mitigates all these things, and it offers a continuing vision of our better, purer selves, and of the better, purer world we could create."

The world we *can* create—if we choose to.[19]

Chapter 7

Faith
under
Siege

*"The dogmas of the quiet past are inadequate
to the stormy present. . . . We must disenthrall
ourselves, and then we shall save our country."*
—Abraham Lincoln

EARLY IN HIS BRIEF PRESIDENCY, JOHN F. KENNEDY FLEW
to France to meet his counterpart, the formidable
Charles de Gaulle. The young president and the old
general had much in common. Both were heroic veterans of World War II and democratically elected leaders
of great nations. Both were not only Christians, but
Roman Catholics, which conceivably suggested their

agreement about how political leaders might be faithful to God and man alike.

But the cautious young American was shaken by the meeting, remarking afterward that the old general held the serene belief that no matter how nations and their leaders blundered by action or inaction, God could be trusted to work things out in the end, making right what humankind makes wrong, and saving us from ourselves.

Ultimately that is the American faith as well, but it does not sit well with us. As a people we are more inclined to operate on the premise that God helps those who help themselves and confirms our righteousness with success. Which explains why George W. Bush did not pause after the September 2001 terrorist attacks on New York and Washington, D.C., to ask himself what Jesus would do in his situation. Wrapping himself in the flag rather than the scriptures, he appealed to patriotism and called the nation to arms, to meet violence with violence.

Nevertheless, on the third day after the attacks, the president ascended the pulpit of Washington National Cathedral to state the nation's case in the form of a remarkable sermon. "Our responsibility to history is already clear," he said. Like popes of old, he called for a crusade to "rid the world of evil."

Then he spoke as the nation's pastor:

> God's signs are not always the ones we look for. We learn in tragedy that his purposes are not always our own, yet the prayers of private suffering . . . are known and heard and understood. . . . The world He created is of moral design. Grief and tragedy and

hatred are only for a time. Goodness, remembrance, and love have no end, and the Lord of life holds all who die and all who mourn. . . . In this trial, we have been reminded and the world has seen that our fellow Americans are generous and kind, resourceful and brave.

The president closed by offering a prayer for the nation, borrowing lines from St. Paul:

We ask almighty God to watch over our nation and grant us patience and resolve in all that is to come. . . . As we've been assured, neither death nor life, nor angels nor principalities, nor powers, nor things present, nor things to come, nor height, nor depth can separate us from God's love. May he bless the souls of the departed. May he comfort our own. And may He always guide our country. God bless America.[1]

It was an extraordinary performance by a political leader, confident in assuming the role of the nation's pastor, as well as prophet of the lingering American faith in God and nation. No elected official of any other democratic nation could have presumed to assume these multiple roles, and the president was uniformly praised for doing so.

The Grapes of Wrath

If there was one discordant note in this remarkable expression of the nation's common creed, it came at the end of the service, when the vast congregation raised its voice in one of the strangest compositions ever to be called a hymn—Julia Ward Howe's "Battle Hymn of the Republic":

> Mine eyes have seen the glory of the coming
>   of the Lord;
> He is trampling out the vintage where the grapes
>   of wrath are stored;
> He hath loosed the fateful lightning of his terrible
>   swift sword;
> His truth is marching on.

The hymn's closing line compares the nation's cause to the sufferings of Christ—"As He died to make men holy, let us die to make men free"—which prompts the question: in times of trial, does the nation follow the God of wrath or the God of love? The terrorists acted in the name of a vengeful God. Would we do the same?

Political leaders were quick to insist that our quarrel was not with Islam but with terrorism. Still, no one could escape the realization that the nation's new enemies draw their righteousness from their religious faith. For the first time since the medieval Crusades, Christians were being denounced as infidels by adherents of another major religion. The suicidal terrorist Mohamed Atta left behind five pages of meditations that stated his case, among them:

> If God supports you, no one will be able to defeat you.
>   God, I trust in you. God, I lay myself in your hands. I ask with the light of your faith that has lit the whole world and lightened all darkness on this earth, to guide me until you approve of me. . . .

Everybody hates death, fears death. But only those, the believers who know the life after death and the reward after death, [are] the ones who will be seeking death.[2]

In the midst of America's own Civil War Abraham Lincoln prophesied that "the dogmas of the quiet past are inadequate to the stormy present." In his second inaugural address he grieved that the domestic conflict was between brothers of the same faith: "Both read the same Bible and pray to the same God, and each invokes his aid against the other."[3]

On that occasion, Lincoln warned:

The prayers of both could not be answered—that of neither has been answered fully. The Almighty has his own purposes. . . .[4]

Faith and the Flag

Much as we wished to think otherwise, on September 11, 2001, America entered a religious war between peoples equally persuaded that God is on their side and against their enemy's.

Of course, religious wars are no novelty, nor is religious persecution unknown in America itself. Over centuries, in defense of orthodoxy, millions of Christians were executed for heresy or died in the wars between Protestants and Catholics. Jews were persecuted simply for being Jews. Our own Puritan forebears, determined to build a New Jerusalem in the New World, were quick to banish or execute anyone with a different take on religious orthodoxy. The Ku Klux Klan burned crosses in an attempt to justify racist hatred by religious faith.

In the wake of the terrorist attacks, the nation sought solidarity in the Stars and Stripes, ignoring Samuel Johnson's warning that patriotism is the last refuge of scoundrels. "God Bless America" fast became the nation's unofficial anthem, affirming the righteousness of our cause. The nation's vaunted separation of church and state was put on hold for the duration of the conflict, because many sensed that what remains of religious faith sustains our public purpose.

After a public school in Rocklin, California, collected $4,000 for victims' families in New York and Washington, D.C., it posted the words "God bless America" on a theater-style marquee on school property. When the American Civil Liberties Union objected to equating patriotic fervor with religious faith, the city's government responded by posting "God bless America" on other public buildings. Across the nation flags flew from auto aerials and church towers.

War unexpectedly inspires poetry. Recall Kipling in the Crimean War and Wilfred Owen in the First World War. Walt Whitman celebrated the terrors of our own Civil War. But in the wake of September 11, America's own poet laureate was unable to compress the national sense of outrage, fear, and righteousness into verse that expresses our public faith.

No wonder: the nation's faith was fuzzy to start with, benignly relying on God's special benevolence to us as a people, and on a sense of our own innocence. When suddenly we were confronted with an evil that draws its justification from a rigorous religious faith, we were collectively befuddled. Overnight our trust in the goodness of human nature was diminished.

The nation's publishers were quick to respond to the national confusion. Philip Yancey's classic, *Where Is God When It Hurts?*, was quickly reprinted and sold 770,000 copies virtually overnight. For a time churches were packed with people seeking solace. Newsmagazines attempted to answer the question, Why do they hate us? Pundits were not at a loss for words, some suggesting that we brought the conflict on ourselves by our political arrogance and cultural decadence. These naysayers were condemned as unpatriotic. From England John le Carre reminded Americans that it was Christendom that originally launched the bloody Crusades against the Muslim "infidels," and Christians, incidentally, who came out the losers of those "holy" wars.[5] In the wake of 9/11, religious pacifists quoting Gandhi, Nelson Mandela, and Dr. King on nonviolence were popularly dismissed as dreamers.

Unsure where to locate the international network of terrorists, the United States bombed a Muslim nation, Afghanistan, that had harbored the extremists' leaders, but were quick to state that we had no quarrel with Islam or the Afghan people. To underscore that message our military dropped seventy thousand daily food parcels to the Afghan people. But early in the war as many as 7.5 million Afghan civilians were forced from their homes and were facing starvation.

Infidels

It soon became apparent that Islamic fundamentalists hold no particular grudge against other religious faiths. Rather, they consider Christians to be unfaithful to Christianity. Like puritans of any faith, Muslim extremists are strict constructionists. When they look at America they do not see a nation of churchgoers, but a people who worship Hollywood, fashion, gossip, games, diets, and sexual license, and whose charity does not extend widely to the largely Islamic developing nations.

In short, their complaint is not with Christianity but with secularism, the West's inheritance from the Enlightenment, which gave us our freedoms, but at the cost of making man, not God, the measure of all things.

It is precisely because the American Dream of a just and caring society has lost its religious roots that radical Islam feels justified in considering Americans to be infidels—unfaithful to the faith we blithely profess but ignore in practice. The Islamic fundamentalists' quarrel is not with Christianity but with the American popular culture of permissiveness, which they find seductive, ungodly, and hypocritical. The America they see is a nation that glories not in God but in *Baywatch*.

Equality, freedom, and individualism are values America inherited not from the Age of Faith but from the Age of Reason.

In America tolerance is a high virtue, but Islamic fundamentalism finds much of American culture to be *in*tolerable, and individualism an affront to the Creator.

The focus of Islamic faith is obedience to God and holy law. A Muslim believer is "faithful" by virtue of submission to God's will. By contrast, Christianity holds that offenses are forgiven as long as one repents. A good Muslim is one who keeps the rules, whereas the self-described "good" Christian may merely acknowledge God and seek his pardon. The contrast of religious cultures is combustible. In the eyes of radical Islam, the prevailing religious faith allows Americans to be permissive in our moral lives.

Samuel Huntington's book *The Clash of Civilizations and the Remaking of the World Order* was widely quoted in the aftermath of the terrorist attacks. "In my view," Huntington noted, "America's greatest sins toward the Arab world are sins of omission." British social critic Melanie Phillips argued that the West maintains an intolerant colonial attitude toward developing nations, "pushing its own values down the throats of non-Western peoples on the grounds that freedom and democracy are superior to the alternatives and must be imposed on the whole world. The West," she proposed, "should end its 'liberal' imperialism and stop telling other cultures how to behave. Instead, it must vigorously defend and reassert liberal values on its home ground. That means, first and foremost, a reassertion of Christianity and an end to the craven apologetics and moral cultural relativism" of the mainstream Protestant churches.[6]

What a Difference a Day Makes

How can we account for the self-indulgence and loss of innocence that Laura Bush identified among Americans? For one thing, an unhappy consequence of the Cold War's end was a sharp drop in news coverage of developing nations and American understanding of the plight of peoples locked in poverty and gagged by repressive regimes. In the 1990s American newspapers and networks closed foreign bureaus as unnecessary expenses.

The *Los Angeles Times* notes that coverage of world news shrank by 70 to 80 percent in response to corporate demands for profits, further reducing Americans' grasp of what was going on beyond our borders.[7] Out of sight, out of mind. *National Geographic* revealed that four out of five Americans could not identify Japan on a world map, and one-fifth couldn't locate the United States in relation to other countries.[8]

In short, Americans were not only ignorant of their faith but of the world. The eminent historian David Nasaw acknowledged that "there is no excusing what happened, but we will never be able to understand this problem until we understand where it came from. No one wants to talk about the origin of the Taliban and the ways in which it's an American creation. We armed it . . . . We destabilized an entire region, and we created this monster."[9]

At the same time that commentators were being silenced for suggesting that American carelessness may have contributed to terrorism, there was a throttling of patriotic free expression on some college campuses. Prominent display of the flag was either discouraged or forbidden as politically incorrect jingoism by authorities.

Accustomed as we were to religious tolerance and quiet displays of faith, Americans were shocked by 9/11 into a new realization of the power of religious faith to motivate people not only to action but to violence. Whereas Christianity and Judaism remain private faith options in America, Islam defines a total way of life for Muslims, regardless of what country they live in. As Princeton historian Bernard Lewis notes, America is a nation subdivided into religious groups, whereas Islam is a "religion subdivided into nations"— a vast and demanding faith, binding its believers more closely than even Christianity did the peoples of Europe in the Age of Faith. Christendom as an entity no longer exists, but Islam does.[10]

Lewis notes that poverty and tyranny in the Muslim world are attributed to "American economic dominance and exploitation, now thinly disguised as 'globalization';" and "to America's support for the many so-called Muslim tyrants who serve its purposes."

The Inadequacy of Private Religion

When a great nation is attacked not only physically but morally, neither patriotism nor a purely private religious faith is adequate to make sense of the world and Americans' responsibilities in it. If Lincoln was correct, and past dogmas are no longer adequate, what will take their place? And how shall we disenthrall ourselves? The occasion cries out for solidarity in faith.

Sociologist Alan Wolfe acknowledges that half of all Americans continue to maintain an absolute sense of morality based on religious faith and believe that "America has become far too atheistic and needs a return to strong religious beliefs." But he adds:

> Just because people think that faith is important does not necessarily mean that they think America has slipped into the hands of secular humanists and requires more public affirmations of religious belief.

For Wolfe, "the compelling question is not whether they think religion is good for them—nearly everyone thinks that it is—but whether they think it is good for others."[11]

In short, do those who retain a firm faith have the right to impose their sense of right and wrong on others? Even strong believers are hesitant to do so, the sociologist notes, because they have raised tolerance to a high civic virtue. Unfortunately, a quiet, private faith does not make for a consensus on national policy. When experts gathered at the Brookings Institution in Washington, D.C., after 9/11 to press for peace between Israel and the Palestinian Authority, they worried that such pressure might look like we were pandering to the Muslim nations. The distinguished Quaker Landrum Bolling brushed away the objections. "We should do it because it's right," he said.

"To exclude, to condemn, is to judge," Wolfe notes, "and middle-class Americans are reluctant to pass judgment on how other people act and think."[12] But the unhappy companion of tolerance is non-involvement. Keeping one's religious faith to oneself has resulted in wholesale retreat from arenas where decisions are made and values are maintained. Toleration of others with whom we disagree too often has become just another name for indifference to them and an excuse for inaction.

Disconnecting

Robert D. Putnam worries that over the past quarter-century Americans have become disconnected from one another. Among the victims are public discourse and shared faith and values. A nation of joiners has slowly but surely become a society of individuals going it alone.

Putnam warns that the shrinkage of socializing is a threat to the nation's civic and personal health and public discourse. Family, friends, and neighbors no longer interact as they once did. Membership in church, PTA, recreation clubs, and political parties has plummeted. Americans are less and less involved with one another, prompting an erosion in quality of life for all and a fractionating of faith and values. Marriage, as we have noted earlier, has become a minority lifestyle, outstripped by those who only cohabit or live alone or live in households with children but no spouse. Putnam insists that marriage has more than romantic value. It socializes and civilizes couples, supports faith and values, and makes men and women more secure financially and responsible for others. As for democracy, Putnam notes that it is not simply a matter of voting but a function of taking joint responsibility for realizing the American Dream.[13]

Nonjoiners experience poorer health and educational performance and more teen pregnancy, child suicide, low birth weight, prenatal mortality, and crime. Americans, once the greatest joiners in the world, have become nesters, keeping company with television rather than real people, preferring virtual reality to flesh-and-blood humanity.

It was not always so. When the republic was still young, de Tocqueville remarked with admiration that

> Americans of all ages, all stations in life, and all types of disposition are forever forming associations. There are not only commercial and industrial associations in which all take part, but others of a thousand different types—religious, moral, serious, futile, very general and very limited, immensely large and very minute.

The young Frenchman concluded: "Nothing, in my view, deserves more attention than the intellectual and moral associations in America."[14]

Despite the shrinkage of faith and socialization, nearly one-half of all social memberships in America remain faith-based, and one-half of all personal philanthropy and volunteer work is church-related. Americans remain more involved with one another by dint of religious faith than by any other relationship outside the family. Churches also serve as homes for other helping associations, from Boy Scouts to Alcoholics Anonymous, supporting their values.

Moreover, churchgoers learn social and leadership skills that translate into other forms of community involvement. Americans of faith vote more regularly, visit friends and entertain at home more often, give more of their time and money to charity, and participate in other interest groups more widely. "Connectedness, not merely faith, is responsible for the beneficence of church people," Putnam notes.[15]

C. Eric Lincoln, a sociologist of religion, notes that for black Americans the church remains "the mother of our culture, the champion of our freedom, and hallmark of our civilization."[16] Despite the decline in faith and observance, church, synagogue, temple, and mosque continue to serve a similar function for Americans of other races and faiths. Although religious tolerance and interfaith cooperation has grown, our understanding of other denominations and faiths lags far behind—not just shallow but practically nonexistent. Islam, which will soon replace Judaism as the nation's second faith, is still a mystery to most Americans.

Privatized Faith

The downside of privatized religion is that it transforms believers into spiritual hermits, responsible only to themselves. Putnam worries that, among those Americans who are still religiously observant, "more people are 'surfing' from congregation to congregation more frequently, so that while they may still be 'religious,' they are less committed to a particular community of believers."[17] Roof notes that "privatized religion knows little of communal support, and exists by and large independent of institutionalized religious forms; it may provide meaning to the believer and personal orientation, but it is not a shared faith, and thus not likely to inspire strong group involvement." He depicts Americans as "'believers' yes, but 'belongers' no."[18]

My own Quaker meeting outside Washington, D.C., illustrates this tenuous hold on faith and community. Only a minority of our attenders become members. The majority drift in and out from Sunday to Sunday, styling themselves as "seekers" rather than believers, content to seek solace, not an informed and committed faith. Often they arrive either wounded in their personal or professional lives, or disillusioned by their experiences with other churches. Typically, they are single or separated. If married, they are not joined or supported in faith by their spouse. Their testimony is sentimental, not religious. Drawn to silent worship, they seek inspiration rather than decision. The former Clerk of our Meeting (the equivalent of minister) confided that we are in danger of becoming "a colloquy of lost souls."[19]

Due to birthrate and immigration, America's Catholic population is increasing, but Putnam notes that "more and more Catholics are becoming merely nominal church members, while a large and steadily growing number of Protestants and Jews are abandoning their religion entirely."[20] Black Americans have traditionally been more religiously observant than whites, but their decline in church attendance between the mid-1970s and mid-1990s nearly matched that of white Americans.

The relative decline in observance among mainline Protestants, as well as Catholics and Jews, has occurred at the same time as a surge in growth among evangelical congregations. Unfortunately, evangelicals tend to confine their involvement within their own religious communities rather than minister to the wider community. Religious faith no longer translates as it once did into a powerful motive for community service. Evangelicals are 75 percent more generous than mainline Protestants in their personal philanthropy, but much of that generosity is restricted to supporting their own churches. In sum, sociologist Robert Wuthnow notes that "mainline Protestant churches encourage civic engagement in the wider community, whereas evangelical churches apparently do not."[21]

He concludes that "religion may have a salutary effect on civil society by encouraging its members to worship, spend time with their families, and to learn the moral lessons embedded in religious traditions. But religion is likely to have a diminished impact on society if that is the only role it plays."[22] In short, what remains of religious faith is fast losing its traditional power to support the American Dream.

Quiet Belief

Abraham Lincoln was prophetic when he cautioned about the inadequacy of past dogmas. But today many Americans have raised tolerance to such a high status that we resist dogma altogether, preferring agnosticism. Lincoln confronted a civil war that pitted coreligionists against one another, and in which aggressors and victims alike were all Americans of faith. Today, most middle-class Americans believe that conflicts can be avoided as long as they keep their faith and consciences to themselves and refrain from inflicting them on others.

For example, a majority of Americans say that while they would not countenance abortion themselves, they prefer not to judge or oppose others who do. Alan Wolfe's research similarly showed that those Americans who believed homosexuals were "born that way" (as opposed to *choosing* to be gay) tended not to condone their behavior, but nevertheless respected gays as individuals.

Wolfe characterizes this new nonjudgmentalism as "quiet belief." Tommy Fasano, a Jehovah's Witness in California, is a strong religious believer, but not an absolutist. He told Wolfe, "I am not here to judge anyone." Believers like Fasano, Wolfe notes, "would not object, and some would be quite pleased, if a pastor or rabbi advised a woman, in private, that abortion was wrong. To do so in public, and in a way not directed toward a particular person but as a general moral injunction to all, whatever their circumstances, that strikes of poking your nose into other people's business."[23]

By raising tolerance and individualism to the status of preeminent virtues, Americans of faith have denied any role for religion in guiding public morality. Still, most Americans believe that the federal government is not at all hostile to their personal religious beliefs and practices. Quiet believers hold that the only fair and practical way to fulfill their religious responsibilities to others is by personal example, not by preaching. In Wolfe's survey more than four out of five Americans who expressed an opinion held that "there are many different religious truths and we ought to be tolerant of all of them."[24]

Tolerance and individualism rest on Americans thinking well of themselves and one another. The events of September 11, 2001, challenged that sunny sense of human nature, as Americans were confronted with evil cloaked in religious righteousness. It is too early to determine whether this disillusionment will make us more suspicious of one another. The surge of patriotism that followed the tragedies seemed to suggest otherwise, provoking solidarity rather than suspicion. Being the victims of foreigners seemed to strengthen Americans' collective sense of personal innocence.

However, as recently as 1990, fewer than four of five Americans expressed a great deal of confidence in their religious *institutions*, whereas nearly all trusted their personal faith.[25]

How We Got This Way

"There is one thing a professor can be absolutely certain of," the humanist Allan Bloom reveals. "Almost every student entering the university believes, or says he believes, that truth is relative. . . . The danger they have been taught to fear from absolutism is not error but intolerance. Relativism is necessary to openness; and this is the virtue, the only virtue, which all primary education for more than fifty years has dedicated itself to inculcating."[26] By and large, students are not truth-seekers, but tolerators.

The older view of what it meant to be American, Bloom argues, was that "by recognizing and accepting man's natural rights, men found a fundamental basis of unity and sameness." Natural rights made us all brothers and sisters. People of faith were persuaded that it was God who gave us those rights and our dignity. Human rights were the basis for the social contract that underlay our shared goals and our vision of the public good and moral order. By contrast, today we have become suspicious of anyone who claims to have some knowledge of the truth, because we equate conviction with intolerance and repression.

It was Lincoln's own conviction that human dignity, instilled by the Creator, was incompatible with slavery, and the president risked the mutual slaughter of Americans to affirm that dogma. Lincoln was neither open nor tolerant of those who, in the name of individualism, chose to hold others in bondage. A century later, civil rights activists demonstrated that black Americans were still held in bondage through racism. They were right, and they persuaded the rest of us that they were right.

The newer "openness" teaches that faiths are merely prejudices, to be tolerated as long as they are held privately and not carried into the public arena. Instead of seeking, holding, and living by truth, an increasing number of Americans opt for their own cultural and moral lifestyles, embracing them as fashions rather than enduring truths. What they *feel* trumps what they believe and know.

Recently, when I lectured on religious faith and practice at a distinguished church-sponsored college, students majoring in religious studies were put off that I expressed my religious convictions without qualification, observing that people act according to their beliefs, not in the absence of belief. When I suggested that Christianity, in the completeness of its revelation, possesses advantages over other faiths, some students politely dismissed me as prejudiced.

CAN THE AMERICAN DREAM ENDURE IN A NATION OF fractionated and fuzzy faiths, permissive individualism, and declining church membership and attendance? Will a litigious society that seldom socializes or serves the community continue to pursue the Dream of a just and generous society for all its members? Will faith trump mere tolerance? Will the commonwealth prevail over personal well-being?

Perhaps. But peace and good will, proclaimed at the birth of the Savior, requires more than God's gratuitous blessing on America. It rests on our solidarity in faith, hope, and love.

Chapter 8

The
Challenge
to the
Churches

"To see that no pain is unshared, no hurt unnoticed,
no hunger untouched, no loss grieved alone,
no death unknown, and no joy uncelebrated."
—Loren B. Mead

GRANTING THE RELATIVE SHALLOWNESS OF RELIGIOUS FAITH
in contemporary America, we are still—overwhelmingly—a believing nation. So what accounts for the
precipitous decline in religious practice over the past
half-century? Could it be that, as the American people
have became more educated, they have become more
skeptical of religion?

In a nationwide study of Presbyterian Baby Boomers, researchers discovered to the contrary that "the amount of formal education has no bearing on how active one is in church. . . . Most of those who lost their faith, or who adopted unorthodox opinions, did so *before*, not after, going to college."[1]

Thomas C. Reeves concurs: "Very few people who leave their churches cite lack of intellectual respectability among their reasons. Pride, indifference, alternative religions, and a wide assortment of diversions may keep some of the educated from Christianity, but the faith itself, as history richly reveals, is not a natural enemy of intellect."[2]

Nor have the Boomers abandoned religious practice because they perceive religion to be intolerant of their relaxed lifestyles. Fully 70 percent of those surveyed by pollsters in 1992 actually favored a "return to stricter moral standards."[3] When Gallup asked people why they attended church less frequently, only 8 percent complained that they disagreed with church teachings. The leading reasons given by the dropouts were "Have no time, too busy" and "Conflicts with work, study schedule," along with "Move around too much, new to community."[4]

In 1991 the Presbyterian Church (USA) in two nationwide polls discovered that more than 60 percent of unchurched people excused their absence not because of any hostility, but because of work and school commitments: "Just a habit/Lazy/Just don't," and "No time." Reeves concludes from the many polls that "great numbers of people stay away from their churches simply because they do not see them as relevant to their lives." To which Gallup adds that the vast majority of Americans are simply not convinced that churchgoing is necessary to be a good Christian.[5]

But Gallup also discovered that mobile Americans tend to be church dropouts because, when they move, few of them are extended an invitation to attend a church in the new community. Of those who *are* invited to join a church, about one-half do. The mainline Protestant denominations in particular are notoriously shy about "evangelizing" their new neighbors when all they need to do is invite and welcome them.[6]

What Americans Expect from Religion

On the basis of his studies, Gallup concludes that Christians want "to deepen their relationships to Jesus Christ" and learn about the Bible. "They also want their churches to help them learn how to put their faith into practice; to shed light on the important moral issues of the day; to help them learn how to serve others better and to be better parents."[7] But Dean Kelley, in his book *Why Conservative Churches Are Growing*, raps the mainline churches for their "placidity, decorum, and tolerance—i.e., sterility" and for failing to meet the spiritual needs of an increasingly dysfunctional secular society.[8]

Sociologists Roger Finke and Rodney Stark agree that successful churches both give much and demand much from their members: "To the degree that denominations reject traditional doctrines and cease to make serious demands on their followers, they cease to prosper. . . . People tend to value religion on the basis of how costly it is to belong—the more one must sacrifice in order to be in good standing, the more valuable the religion."[9]

If Americans have the perception that churchgoing has nothing to do with their being good Christians, then the churches are failing to offer something more—and other—than the secular culture provides. "In the last analysis," a British evangelical alliance reflected about that overwhelmingly unchurched nation, "there is only one distinction to be made; that is, between those who believe in the essentials of the Gospel and those who do not. This fundamental distinction is drawn sharply in the New Testament, as sharply as the difference between darkness and light, death and life."[10]

The late British commentator Malcolm Muggeridge contrasted religious culture with that of the world. "We become forgetful," he observed, "that Jesus is the prophet of the losers' not the victors' camp, the one who proclaims that the first will be last, that the weak are the strong, and the fools are the wise."[11] This is not a message much heard from the nation's pulpits.

It is not as if heavy doses of theology are necessary to deepen the faith of Americans. Jesus explained the truth through stories everyone can understand. And, as Reeves notes, "everyone can understand pleas for personal integrity, marital fidelity, sensitivity and respect for others."[12]

It does not help that religion is practically invisible in the popular culture, prompting television journalist Bill Moyers to comment, "Just about every other human endeavor is the subject of continuing coverage by the media, even to the point of saturation," whereas there is "no room at the inn" for religion as a "crucial force in American life. So most Americans remain religiously illiterate."[13]

Several years ago, when I was first invited to submit a weekly column for a national syndicate, my editors advised that it would be welcomed by more local newspapers as a "lifestyle" piece rather than one clearly about religion. When religious faith is reduced to just another lifestyle, we know the churches are failing at their job.

Morality Flows from Faith

A mile wide, inch deep faith cannot sustain a moral nation. Muggeridge observed that "the movement away from Christian moral standards has not meant moving to an alternative humanistic system of moral standards as was anticipated, but moving into a moral vacuum." Even President Clinton acknowledged the link between religious observance and moral health in America. In 1995 he asked publicly: "Don't you believe that if every kid in every difficult neighborhood in America were in a religious institution on weekends . . . don't you believe that the drug rate, the crime rate, the violence rate, the sense of self-destruction would go way down and the quality and character of this country would go way up?"[14]

Some of the blame for the erosion of faith and practice must be laid at the feet of the clergy. Gallup discovered that nearly one in five of unchurched Americans dropped out because of "a bad experience with a pastor." "The people who come to church on Sundays are not by definition, as some clergy think, the enemy," Reeves comments. "Some might even become, if at all encouraged, friends."[15] But sermons are notoriously short on teaching the fundamentals of faith. What man of you, said Jesus, "if his son asks him for bread, will give him a stone? Or if he asks for a fish, will give him a serpent?" (Matthew 7:9-10).

"If mainline Christians know more about professional sports or soap operas than about their religion," Reeves concludes, "it is at least in part because they have not been taught." Of clergy, he notes, "In no other profession, except for the professorate, is the temptation to be lazy as easily indulged."[16]

Above all, faith teaches respect for people. If the faith be true, C. S. Lewis insisted, "there are no *ordinary* people. You have never talked to a mere mortal. Nations, cultures, arts, civilization—these are mortal, and their life is to ours as the life of a gnat. But it is immortals whom we joke with, work with, marry, snub, and exploit—immortal horrors or everlasting splendors."[17]

A Fall from Grace

If there were any doubts about the potential impact of clergy sex abuse scandals on the nation's Roman Catholics, they were answered in a Gallup poll taken in mid-2002. Whereas 59 percent of Protestants continued to express "a great deal" or "quite a lot" of confidence in organized religion, only 42 percent of American Catholics agreed.[18]

Four in ten Catholics acknowledged that they were contributing less money to the church because of the scandals. In 2002 fewer than one-third of Catholics admitted to being weekly churchgoers, a nearly 30 percent decline since the abuses were first reported. In the 1950s and 1960s, fully three-fourths of American Catholics worshiped every week. But by 2002, for the first time in history, the percentage of Catholic church attendance dropped below that of Protestants.[19]

Overall, in 2001 nearly two-thirds of all citizens gave very high or high ratings to the ethical standards of clergy. But by mid-2002 only slightly more than one-half of Americans maintained the same level of esteem.[20]

For more than sixty years the Gallup organization has provided an annual index of the nation's religiosity based on eight measurements of faith and practice. That index reached its lowest ebb ever in 2002—641 of a possible 1,000 points—a 30-point drop from the previous year.[21]

Still, despite disenchantment, some measures of individual religiosity remain constant and strong. An overwhelming 95 percent of Americans continue to profess a belief in God. Nine of ten freely reveal their religious preference, and two-thirds hold membership in a denomination. Although sociologists dispute actual attendance figures, 43 percent of Americans still tell pollsters that they attended church within the previous week.[22]

Three of five Americans insist that religion is very important in their lives. Even more believe that religion answers their problems. A Gallup survey in 2000 revealed that nearly two-thirds of Americans concede that their religious beliefs not only keep them from acting immorally but spur them to volunteer time and money to the needy. And eight in ten Americans say that their religious faith helps them not only to respect and assist other people, but to respect people of other faiths. Faith, moreover, feeds self-respect.[23]

The faith of Americans is vulnerable to disenchantment because it is shallow and largely unsupported. While two-thirds of citizens believe that the Bible answers all or most of the basic questions of life, the percentage of Americans who admit to rarely or never reading the Bible actually doubled during the 1990s to 41 percent. The overwhelming excuses were "just not interested," "no time," and "not a religious person."[24]

Paradoxically, early in the same decade, the percentage of Americans who say they would like to experience spiritual growth in their lives actually increased by one-third—to eight of every ten citizens. Gallup worries that "much of the spirituality today appears to be ungrounded in teachings, tradition, or Scripture. . . . Americans, little aware of their own religious traditions, are practicing a do-it-yourself, 'whatever works' kind of religion, picking and choosing among beliefs and practices of various faith traditions."[25]

Today nearly one-half of Americans describe themselves as "born again" or evangelical.[26] Nevertheless, on the basis of his surveys, Gallup concludes that, despite good intentions, no more than 13 percent of Americans possess a truly integrated, transforming faith, with "a solid commitment to God and lived out in service to others."[27]

There is no excuse for "do-it-yourself" faiths based on ignorance and mere good intentions. It is the churches' challenge to teach, to implore, to motivate, to call to service, and to assist Americans to grow in faith.

Meeting the Challenge
Kenneth Kantzer argues that "no church can be effective to bring clarity and commitment to a world when it is ignorant of its own basic principles as our church is today. And, unless we engage the church in a mighty program of reeducation, it will be unable to transmit a

Christian heritage to its own children or the society around it."[28]

English evangelist John R. W. Stott adds that the church must not only teach but listen. "The best preachers," he acknowledges, "know the people . . . and understand the human scene in all its pain and pleasure, glory and tragedy. And the quickest way for us to gain such an understanding is to shut our mouths . . . and open our eyes and ears. . . . We need, then, to ask people questions and get them talking."[29]

So the church's challenge starts with improving communication. Unfortunately, the American public resists information that is not entertaining. In 2002 the American Booksellers Association revealed that eight out of ten Americans neither bought nor read a book that year. Indeed, nearly three out of five Americans haven't opened a book since high school, and 42 percent of college graduates haven't read any book, fiction or nonfiction, since they graduated.[30]

Sociologists Dean R. Hoge, Benton Johnson, and Donald A. Luidens worry that the churches will "change their goals for the sake of preserving their budgets and structures. . . . Some incumbents will argue for changing the goals, not the institutions. That temptation must be rejected. The mission and goals of the church are based in scripture and must be kept unchanged."[31]

They argue that ministering to Baby Boomers is different from ministering to their elders:

Baby Boomers have a market view of churches. Boomers see churches as selling a product which they are free to buy or not to buy as they wish, and they feel perfectly free to change from one supplier to another if there is a reason to do so. Most feel no obligation to participate in churches at all, either because they are skeptical about one or another church teaching or because they are convinced that "you don't have to go to church to be a good Christian." Either way, they feel no obligation.[32]

Nevertheless, the researchers discovered that Americans are in the market for some commodities that the churches are in a position to offer. Remarkably, 96 percent of both churched and unchurched Americans in their survey wanted religious education for their children. Many said they also sought personal support and reassurance. Large numbers look to churches to satisfy their need for social contacts and a sense of community. They also value inspiration and spiritual guidance, for "worship to be uplifting and empowering, drawing them away from petty concerns to remember the larger picture, out of self-pity to praise, adoration, and thanksgiving."[33]

The sociologists found their respondents largely inarticulate about their search for meaning in life, yet prone to acknowledge that "churches are a primary place to turn to when facing ultimate questions" and admitting that "no one else in our society deals in this commodity."[34]

These are needs the churches can meet, but not passively. Rather, they must possess authority if their answers are to be not just emotionally uplifting, but recognized as true. Unfortunately, authority in the Catholic church has been eroding since the Second Vatican Council of the 1960s, and Protestantism was born of protest against church authority. Only fundamentalist denominations find literal authority in the Scriptures.

Sociologist Donald Miller notes that the fast-growing megachurches in Southern California profess strong biblical authority. However:

> The pastor gives a personal perspective on any passage and then invites the members to study, pray, ask for inspiration from the Holy Spirit, and decide for themselves. The pastor tells the people, "You read the Bible yourself! You may come out at a different place from me. This is how I read it, but you need to read it for yourself." No one tries to adjudicate individual differences. The authority of the biblical passages comes from a combination of historical text and personal ratification by the Holy Spirit. Thus biblical authority is maintained at a certain level.[35]

What Can Be Done?

Through the Alban Institute that he founded, Loren B. Mead, an Episcopal priest, has devoted his life to revitalizing the American church and its people. In the interests of full disclosure, I will acknowledge that he is a personal friend, and that he and his colleagues helped me professionally some years ago when I was chairman of a seminary whose staff had become dysfunctional. Mead and his colleagues are like country doctors—the ones who still make home visits to make their patients well. The "patients" in his case are churches and congregations of all denominations across America.

Of the nation's churches, he acknowledges, "I honestly do not know if we—as a set of institutions—can survive the difficulties we face."[36] He finds them perversely competitive and impatient, lacking in trust, vision, and a sense of urgency. In a nation characterized by a mile-wide but inch-deep religious faith, he identifies five challenges to which the churches must respond:

- To transfer the ownership of the church
- To discover new structures for the church
- To discover a passionate spirituality
- To make the church a new community and source of community
- To become an apostolic people.

Shifting Ownership

"In America," Mead comments, "the church is owned by its clergy."[37] A lay friend once complained to him: "Sometimes it looks to me as if the church is just an employment agency for clergy!"[38] Even where lay leadership prevails, the clergy "almost always have veto power" and a vested interest in the familiar status quo. Moreover, lay leadership tends to rotate every few years, just when vestrymen, elders, and members of parish councils are learning the ropes—while the clergy stay on indefinitely. Psychology also benefits the clergy, who tend to over-function as "helpers," unwittingly encouraging the laity to under-function and be spiritually dependent.[39]

Mead argues that "the task of the next generations will be to shift the power and ownership of the churches to allow laypeople to fulfill their apostolic ministries and, in so doing, free the clergy to be the catalysts of religious authority."[40]

Finding New Structures

He reflects that "an assumption of suspicion has replaced the assumption of trust" in the structures on which we depend—not just in the church, but in law, medicine, higher education, business, and government as well. "No matter how hard the 'upper' levels try to listen to the 'grassroots,' they are not perceived as being very attentive."[41] Local congregations of different denominations often collaborate easily to serve community needs—supporting food banks, homeless shelters, and retirement home ministries—but at the state, regional, and national levels the denominations tend to focus on their budgets and staffing, not on collaboration. Small, single-pastor congregations that are not completely self-supporting become dependent on subsidies from higher-up.

Mead urges: "We need local congregations operating with less than full-time staff. . . . We need congregations with the courage to merge their operations with others, not necessarily of the same denomination or even faith group."[42] In fact, among churchgoing Americans there is less denominational differentiation than ever, with a constant flow of ordinary Christians from one denomination to another. "Let's be honest," Mead says. "Most of our denominational differences represent territorial and theological feuds now three or four hundred years old." That is not to say that the differences do not matter, but only that "it would be hard to find a nickel's worth of difference between most of the denominations in basic theological principles today."[43]

The differences are more a matter of style and liturgical practice. As for the mission goals of the denominations, they are already consistent with one another:

"Each is concerned for caring for the homeless and hungry in our society. Each worries about those who are excluded from society. . . . Each is trying to learn better to deal with ethnic diversity. . . . Compared to where denominational differences were just a half century ago, we are already 'like family'. . . . What's left to be different about, except aesthetics and memory?"[44]

Moreover, Mead contends, "the church of the future is called to stand beside and with other world faiths, not over them. . . . Can we understand our own faith to be large enough and secure enough not to have to lord it over others?"[45]

Nurturing a Passionate Spirituality

The church has always been uncomfortable with its saints while they were living, because they were not organization men and women, content with creeds and bureaucracies. Rather, the saints nourished powerful, personal, and often life-changing experiences with God. Whereas the institutional church has a corporate relationship with God, its individual members have personal relationships with him. The church would much prefer a laity that stood and knelt on cue and sang from the same hymnal, so it refrains from encouraging what it regards as eccentric.

Mead, growing up in the tradition-laden Episcopal church, remarks that "it was as if the churches and parishioners had an implicit understanding that experiences did not matter in the church or to the church. It felt to us like a collusion of silence."[46]

By contrast, my wife and I worship in a tradition that, while it reveres silence and decorum, is yet open to individual inspiration. Quakers keep quiet, listening for God's voice, until they feel moved to share an emotion or an insight. Some Friends never speak up; some never seem to shut up. But that's human nature. Nevertheless, we value God's ability to connect with each of us in an individual way, as well as with us all corporately. Mead concludes that "a church that does not find a way to include the liveliness of both of these ways of spirituality is likely to miss something that God has in store for all of us. . . . The church is challenged to develop a larger spirituality than it has."[47]

Creating Community

Sociologists worry that Americans over the past quarter-century have become less and less involved in school, sports, clubs, local politics, and other associations that take them out of themselves and give them a sense of belonging and identity. Marrying later and divorcing sooner, many Americans find themselves effectively disengaged, isolated, and on their own.

Through their local congregations the churches have consistently served as extended families, providing community. So it is doubly tragic that churchgoing and community are both in precipitous decline. Mead argues that "the church of the future must become a center within society that feeds and supports the human need for community,"[48] while admitting that "for all too many, congregations appear to be self-satisfied conglomerations of like-minded people."[49] Focus groups of unchurched Americans assembled by the United Methodist church discovered people saying: "I have yet to find a church where people want to be there because of shared values instead of just being cliquish and judgmental."[50]

"Community," says Mead, "is not just a nice product we have to sell to society; it is what we are as Christians."[51] What is encouraging is that church-goers, empowered by their local faith community, are much more inclined to commit themselves to serve the larger community. The pagans remarked of the early Christians: "See how they love one another." To offer the gift of community the congregation must seek out and welcome every stranger and make him and her a brother and sister in the central act of worship:

> Great worship opens hearts to hear the cries of lone-liness and joy of the congregation. Great worship places us with the great pain of the world and of our neighbors, and it sharpens our commitment to making a difference. Great worship helps us celebrate the grandeur and the misery of existence. Great worship makes and should make great demands on us — to be committed to serving God's people and God's world. Great worship brings healing where there is illness, strength where there is weakness, forgiveness where there is guilt. It is the doorway through which God tells us who we are and empowers us to be what God calls us to be.[52]

Becoming an Apostolic People

Mead laments that "in our domestic churches the laity is treated like the overseas clients of the home church's missionary effort; the laity is the pagan, treated as a stranger to the gospel, ignorant of revelation of God, untutored in the ways deemed essential for valid faith and mission."[53]

If faith is to be more than an inch deep it must empower the believer into service. The church must stop exhorting and concentrate on listening to God and God's people. Rather than condemn, it must celebrate and bless, identifying itself (in Mead's words) "with the suffering that creeps into every life, every home, every community. . . . The church is to release its people for service—not direct them or organize them but release them. . . . Instead of proclaiming answers, we need a liturgy of openness and expectation . . . being servants of humanity and the world."[54]

"Can These Bones Live?"

The question was posed by God to Ezekiel (37:3), who answered, "You alone know." Then God explained: "These bones are the whole house of Israel" (37:11).

Can the church, like Israel, be brought back to life? Ezekiel's question was raised in the nineteenth century by John Henry Newman and applied to the moribund Anglican church of his day. Loren Mead raises it again for the church in America in the new millennium:

> The great creative adaptation of the people of Israel began when they discovered that they were living in Babylon. I believe we in the churches are, indeed, in a foreign land, our own Babylon. But too many of us continue to pretend that we are surrounded by the comfortable walls of Jerusalem, safe in the shadow of the temple. Or we think we have only to make a few adjustments to the city wall or the architecture of the temple to return to the comfortable days we think we had in the past. No. The bones really are dry. . . . What we can know is that God is faithful. We

can know that in Babylon God called a lost people, and they responded.[55]

Today it is the churches that are challenged to respond.

Must Churches Grow?

As a rule, before I address congregations, I ask the local clergy whether their membership is stable, growing, or slipping. But I am changing my ways, because I am increasingly aware that membership is not the only measure of a church's vitality. A Lutheran pastor recently suggested to me that a congregation's health is not a function of numbers alone, but of growth in faith and mutual service.

The irreverent British columnist A. A. Gill, criticized for clinging to his Christian faith, said:

Christianity started with 11 members and was at its strongest and purest. If it goes back to being 11, or if I'm the only poor creature in the world left afflicted with it, it will make no difference. God will still be there and will still love us unrequited. The world was still round when nobody believed it.[56]

Mead agrees that some churches can be failures in the numbers game but winners as their members grow in faith and mutual ministry. Ted Buckle, an archdeacon of the Anglican church in New Zealand, suggests that, beyond numerical growth, there are other measures of a church's effectiveness.[57]

Maturational growth: This growth is in stature and maturity of each member, growth in faith and in the ability to nurture and be nurtured.

Organic growth: This is growth of the congregation as a functioning community, able to maintain itself as a living organism; an institution that can engage the other institutions of society.

Incarnational growth: This is growth in the ability to take the meanings and values of the faith-story and make them real in the world and society outside the congregation. The congregation grows in its ability to enflesh in the community what the faith is all about.

Growing in Spirit and Service

Spiritual growth is elusive, because it cannot be taught in a classroom. In seminaries it is referred to as spiritual *formation.* Mead understands spirituality "to involve an open and continuing dialogue between who and what I am with God's intentions and purposes for me. . . . My congregation needs to help me keep it going."[58]

It's not an easy conversation. Our first parents conversed uneasily with God in the Garden of Eden, when they really wanted to be free of him. It is human nature to seek autonomy and independence—to be so in charge of one's own life that we no longer need God. Mead notes that "a congregation that helps you with spiritual development is a congregation that helps you avoid getting stuck."[59]

A vital congregation is one that does not allow itself to get stuck but that makes the liturgical year an adventure and a learning experience. The congregation celebrates or marks its members' most significant events: birth, maturity, marriage, children, illness, and death.

The primary task of the congregation in helping spiritual growth is thus very simple. It is maintaining that steady rhythm of exposure to Scripture and worship week in and week out, year after year. . . . The secondary task of the congregation is to provide skilled help at life's transition points so that dialogue with God occurs and leads us on.[60]

Congregations like to refer to themselves as church "families." Like natural families, they are societies wherein each member is accepted and nurtured, plays a role, and contributes to the others. But churches differ from families in that they are voluntary associations. The bonds in these extended families of faith cannot be taken for granted but must be forged. Those rare congregations that are blessed with numerical growth can become impersonal and unwieldy. They are challenged to grow organically as well.

Growing Organically and Incarnationally

Mead notes that congregations pay inadequate attention to the socialization of their members, prompting fully half of new members to drop out within two years. To allow such disenchantment, he says, is a violation of the church family's own beliefs and values.

They have failed to receive and give hospitality to one of God's children who was seeking to make a home in the community. Congregations cannot spend too much time developing ways to help the newcomer find her or his way into community. This is not an organizational issue alone; it is also a basic issue of the faith.[61]

My wife and I have both devoted extended portions of our careers to fundraising for charitable causes. In our experience, successful fundraisers are known for their faith in the causes they represent and for their persistent cultivation of donors. For a community of faith to grow organically its members must cultivate one another.

But faith communities must also look beyond themselves and grow incarnationally. Congregations have a responsibility to the larger community and to the life of the world. Unfortunately, congregations devoted to "outreach" to the larger society can degenerate into self-serving and self-congratulatory do-gooders.

Mead warns of the temptation

> to make outreach to the oppressed the primary task rather than an expression of a community whose primary task has to do with relationship to God. . . . The better a congregation gets at building up its base as a religious community and sending its people to engage the world, the more it will generate incarnational growth.[62]

Chesterton was fond of excusing his clumsy attempts to translate good intentions into successful action. "Anything worth doing," he concluded, "is worth doing badly."[63] The family that can laugh at its shortcomings is a healthy family. So, too, is the congregation that eschews solemnity and righteousness.

Lamentably, it is the rare seminary that teaches future ministers and priests to cultivate a sense of humor. Yet human nature, even when graced and redeemed, is prone to foible and can be met intelligently only with laughter. St. Paul, who was not known for his hilarity, nevertheless affirmed that believers must be fools for Christ.

The churches would do well to acknowledge a degree of foolishness in the disparity between their aspirations and their accomplishments. Some might consider that disparity to be tragic. In truth, it is comedy of a kind that can redeem each of us and help to realize the American Dream for us all.

Chapter 9

Expanding
the
Dimensions
of
Faith

"*When you scratch an American, he always says:
'This is God's country'. . . . America has become
the substitute for religion.*"
—Norman Mailer, 2002

IN AN ESSAY WRITTEN NOT LONG AFTER WORLD WAR I,
Joseph Wood Krutch mourned the waning of romantic
love following the Victorian era and feared for its consequences. Love, he argued, is a high product of the
human imagination, a relatively late addition to
human history. The Victorians believed love to be the
ultimate purpose in life. Live for love was their motto.[1]

To be sure, love in Victorian practice was often only refined sentiment or even sentimentality rather than the ultimate and sustaining virtue that defines its Christian counterpart. Nevertheless, the Victorians aimed high: for them love was devoted and assumed to be permanent. The wedding band Abraham Lincoln gave his bride, Mary Todd, was inscribed "Love is eternal."

By the early twentieth century these sentiments were already in retreat. The shell of romance remained, but love was no longer assumed to be eternal, nor even a high sentiment. People still yearned for love but did not live for it. By century's end its motivation was no longer assumed to be providential but only natural and accidental, the promptings of one's hormones.

A Dual Loss

Ironically, the sentimentality that formerly characterized romance was transferred to faith, and religious conviction in turn was replaced by an amorphous "spirituality."

That few Americans are discomfited by these dual losses (or are even aware of them) is due to the fact that the great majority of Americans still profess to believe in love and believe in God even as the faiths we articulate and practice no longer support those beliefs. As Norman Mailer noted on the first anniversary of the terrorist attacks on New York and Washington, America has become the substitute for religion.[2] God, having blessed America, is no longer consulted. In his stead we are inclined to worship the American Dream as if it were already realized. In fact, vast numbers of Americans are still excluded from the Dream, which was founded on a religious faith that has long since shifted and eroded.

The Victorian embrace of love as the rule of life reflected, in part, an early erosion of religious faith in that increasingly skeptical age. According to Krutch, in romantic love the Victorians

> found themselves in the presence of something that awoke in them that sense of reverence which nothing else claimed, and something to which they felt, even in the very depths of their being, that an unquestioning loyalty was due. For them love, like God, demanded all sacrifices; but like him, also, it rewarded the believer by investing all the phenomena of life with a meaning not yet analyzed away.[3]

Alas, romantic love proved to be no substitute for God. Since Victorian times, Krutch lamented that "We have grown used—more than they—to a Godless universe, but we are not yet accustomed to one which is loveless as well, and only when we have so become shall we realize what atheism really means."[4]

Few Americans could become accustomed to a Godless universe. But a mile-wide, inch-deep religious faith which, in effect, ignores and trivializes the deity and exerts little impact on the direction of believers' lives is dangerously close to loveless atheism.

Toward the Next Great Awakening

Our nation has enjoyed two great religious revivals, the first in Colonial times, the second spanning the first three decades of the nineteenth century. Another Great Awakening to faith is already long overdue.

Today, despite widespread acknowledgment of God's existence, barely one in five Americans devotes any time or attention to the practice of religious faith.[5] Meanwhile, half the churches across the nation have fewer than seventy-five members, and they are closing at the rate of fifty every week.[6] Happily, the trend can be reversed by a fresh awakening to faith and to faithful service. Here are some ways it can happen:

1. Exchange "spirituality" for religion.

In our times, spirituality has become a free-floating sentiment divorced from religion. One can feel spiritual about a pet, nature, art, or even oneself. At best spirituality is merely sentimental; at worst it amounts to self-worship. Unlike faith, hope, and love, it cannot be shared with others.

Spirituality professes to be humble and unassuming because it is always seeking, morphing, and incomplete. Whereas religion is something else altogether, defining the actual, permanent relationship of every mortal to God—subordinate, dependent, flawed, tested, redeemed, and hopeful. By extension, religion defines our responsibility to one another, not resting on feeling at all, but on conviction, devotion, and gratitude. Religion acknowledges that faith itself is a gift not of our own creation. It puts an end to random seeking in favor of accepting what God has already revealed, however indistinctly we perceive that revelation.

2. Let God be God.

God is love, but he is not benign. People do not define God; he defines himself *and* us. Even a cursory reading of Scripture reveals him to be demanding. Just as the agnostic cannot obscure God by looking the other way, the atheist cannot make him disappear altogether. To return to faith we must let God be God.

Although some believers balk at referring to God as masculine, it is inexcusable to depersonalize him altogether. God is not an "it." If he were, we could not relate to him personally.

Nor is God silent. The Scriptures are at no loss for words—*God's* words. Nor is he elusive. The history of religion is a chronicle of his constant (and often unwelcomed) intrusions.

God is easily dismissed by those who demand, "Where was he when I needed him?" or "How could a good God allow tragedies to befall his creatures?" In each instance the inference is that the creator's alleged indifference makes him evil.

If God were evil, or even indifferent, it is remarkable that people ever came to conceive of him as good, as C. S. Lewis noted. Common sense and experience alike demonstrate that true evil is inflicted by man on man, while Scripture is a record of God's efforts to change men's hearts and save us from ourselves. A trouble-free universe would require fire that warms but does not burn, water that quenches thirst but does not drown, and people so controlled by their Maker that they would have no self-will or personal motivation. What use would the Creator have for mere puppets?

3. Test faith by commitment.

"By their fruit you shall know them" is the perennial truth about religious faith. Everyone must act on faith, not certitude. But sentiment or mere inclination can masquerade as faith. Quakers have no creed to express their beliefs but rely instead on an inner light to inform their consciences. I once asked a wise Friend how to determine whether his inspiration was true or bogus. "Easy enough," he replied. "Judge me not by what I say but by what I *do!*"

Revelation demonstrates that God prefers to deal with groups rather than individuals. Of course, he works through selected individuals, but not for their personal benefit. Rather, he employs them for the people's benefit. He dealt with Israel as a nation and with Christians as an extension of the chosen people. The reasons are clear: God's revelation, his providence, and his promise are the same for all of his creatures. He does not play favorites. We are all of us not just in the same boat, but have the same destination, and we are all expected to pull on the oars.

The earliest Christians worshiped as a community, accepting that the church is an extended family. The perversity of today's mile-wide, inch-deep faith is that it is prized as a personal possession and carries no commitments, but only rewards. Early in its history the church was confronted by Gnostics who thought they possessed secret wisdom unavailable to others. Against them and others who would revise the truth the church articulated a creed that summarized the faith common to all believers.

When eccentrics wandered off as hermits pursuing their own righteousness, the church gathered them into monastic communities where their faith was tested by love and responsibility for one another. For a Great Awakening in our own time we must nourish faith in community.

4. Exchange love for mere sentiment.

A faith based on sentiment will always be limited, whereas a faith based on love is universal. God does not play favorites. He is the great democrat, treating everyone equally, sinners as well as saints. As he is not sentimental, neither ought we to be. Instead we can emulate him in loving service, which is often onerous and bereft of consolation.

People do not have to like others in order to love them, but must accept the fact that God loves others as much as he loves us. We are equally called to service: "What you have done for the least of my brethren you have done to me."

Love is not a feeling but a devoted *doing*.

5. Acknowledge faults and forgive.

Any Great Awakening to faith in our time will require an acknowledgment of frailty. Today only one in four Americans admits to trusting others,[7] but nearly all of us trust ourselves. That can only be because people excuse themselves more easily than they forgive others.

A life of faith cannot be constructed on a foundation of mistrust. Better to return to the fact that we are all not merely frail but inclined to be perverse, proud, and self-indulgent. It is only by acknowledging our faults that we can accept God's forgiveness, which then leaves us free to forgive others.

We are all inclined to persuade ourselves of our innocence when we are merely well-intentioned. Alcoholics and other addicts understand sin better than most, having experienced the damage it has done to them and those they care for. A "recovered" alcoholic acknowledges he is still an alcoholic. Likewise, the redeemed believer wisely acknowledges that he is still vulnerable. Humility is a virtue precisely because it acknowledges the truth about ourselves.

6. Live the Sermon on the Mount.

While working on a book, Pulitzer Prize-winning journalist Tony Horwitz attended a Baptist church in Guthrie, Kentucky. The preacher devoted his two-hour-long sermon to posing this question to his congregation: "If you were arrested and charged for being a Christian, would there be any evidence to convict you?"

Even a second-rate defense attorney could plead successfully that mere church-going is insufficient evidence to support the charge of being a Christian. So, too, is any nominal profession of faith. ("Your honor, you realize the defendant needs to appear to be a Christian to be accepted in this town. But rest assured, his faith is no threat to the community!").

Given the same scenario, any Christian with *real* religious convictions would likely be convicted. I can imagine a clever prosecutor demanding how the defendant regards Jesus's Sermon on the Mount. That's the true test of faith, but it is seldom the subject of preaching in our churches, so it is conveniently ignored.

According to the Sermon, the evidence for being a Christian is that one be simple, humble, truthful, peace-making, generous, persecuted, unassuming, loving, and forgiving—even of one's enemies. By these measures (which are Jesus's own) there are probably not a multitude of Christians around.

Following Jesus's arrest in Gethsemane, the apostle Peter followed at a distance to discover what dire judgment awaited his master. Lest the same fate befall him as well, Peter repeatedly denied that he even knew Jesus—lies that Jesus forewarned Peter that he would tell. Confronted with his own faithlessness, the apostle was moved to remorse. But the story did not end there. Of more importance, Peter recovered, became the apostles' leader, and, at length was executed for his master's sake.

Admittedly, Peter's discipleship is an extreme example that few Christians are called to emulate, but it nevertheless demonstrates authentic religion.

7. Preach the Gospel.
The closest many people of faith come to their clergy is during the weekly sermon or homily. The rest of the time we are largely on our own, attempting to be faithful by our best lights. The weekly sermon is meant to shed light on our lives as a reflection of God's revelation. That is why it is essential to preach the Gospel.

Clergy in America are inclined to advertise their upcoming sermons with catchy titles displayed in large block letters on the announcement boards outside their churches. Too often they resemble newspaper headlines, employing cute double entendres, aimed to draw a chuckle.

Early in my writing career a wise editor advised me to refrain from moralizing in my books, instead reminding readers of what they already know but may have lacked the opportunity to ponder sufficiently or to put into practice. That counsel could be applied to preachers as well. The clergy are well advised not to nag their congregations. Still it is true that consciences need to be informed for people to be effective, and conscience is best formed by the fundamentals of the faith. For Christians that means preaching the Gospel in and out of season.

One need not be a fundamentalist to affirm the fundamentals, nor a revisionist to reaffirm the faith in a manner that is relevant to life in the twenty-first century. The Gospel is as fresh as it was when John the Baptist called for repentance and preached that salvation depends on a change of heart. It has not changed since the Savior repeated the Baptist's call and announced that God was walking again among men as he had with Adam and Eve in the Garden of Eden, and that God's kingdom was at hand.

Laymen might be surprised how little time is set aside in seminary training for learning to preach well. Over the years I have come to suspect that the techniques of effective preaching are given short shrift for fear that clergy will treat the pulpit as a stage and become mere performers.

Vastly more important than technique is the sermon's substance. Jesus himself was effective not because he was a scholar but because he was a storyteller. Just as many people (myself included) are hapless at telling jokes, some clergy are unimaginative story-tellers. Still, they can proclaim the Gospel in Jesus's own words, offering no excuses for repeating them.

A major impediment to effective preaching is that the typical minister is fully occupied with the care of his or her congregation and seldom, if ever, has the opportunity to hear someone else preach. Is it any wonder that sermons soon turn stale? For years I served as chairman of the College of Preachers at

Washington National Cathedral, an institution devoted to renewing the vitality of clergy of all denominations in mid-career, most notably restoring their sense of the Gospel they are commissioned to preach. At the moment I serve as vice-chairman of a group of twelve Protestant and Catholic seminaries dedicated to instilling in future priests and ministers the Gospel message and promise to which they all adhere despite denominational differences. If ecumenism is to succeed in our time and speed a third Great Awakening to faith, it will not be by muting the differences among the denominations, but by proclaiming the same Gospel.

8. Be inclusive.

Every church purports to welcome the inquiring stranger, but most congregations conform to what demographers would call "exclusive communities." As Martin Luther King Jr. lamented, Americans are never so segregated as they are at Sunday worship.

Because the church is an extended family, African Americans, Hispanics, and Asian Americans are predictably attracted to worship in the company of people like themselves. But there is no excuse for prosperous white middle-class congregations to be complacent with their present memberships without making an effort to include the faithful of other ethnicities and economic classes. Jesus pronounced the poor to be blessed, but impoverished Americans are disproportionately unchurched because they are uninvited.

Some congregations will continue to consider homosexuals and lesbians to be living a sinful lifestyle and exclude them from membership or, at the very least, from ministry. On retiring as Archbishop of Canterbury,

George Carey predicted that the issue of homosexuality was likely to split the worldwide Anglican communion. If so, it would make the church the victim of a lifestyle with which it feels uncomfortable.

The reason for Christianity's initial success owed much to its being inclusive. Poor and rich; slave and free; Jew, Roman, and barbarian; men, women, and children of all races and nations were accepted and treated equally. There were no distinctions. All were called and all were welcomed. It was only later, after the church had become established and institutional-ized, that its leaders sought to preserve its "purity" by excluding people—notably heretics and public sin-ners—for fear that they might tempt others among the faithful to their ways.

But even in our permissive times, sexuality is sel-dom public. Adultery, promiscuity, and cohabitation are far more common among Christians than homo-sexuality, yet only rarely are the adulterers and the promiscuous among laity and clergy "outed" as gays are. Instead they worship alongside us and share in communion unimpeded.

Few Americans believe any longer that anyone freely chooses to be gay; some men and women simply are, and many are honest enough to acknowledge their orientation. There is little danger of their tempting others not so oriented to embrace their lifestyle. So why allow the issue to distract the church from its purpose of service and sanctification? If God can for-give, the church can forgive, for its own integrity and preservation.

But what of ordaining gay clergy and blessing homosexual unions? The church is wise to hesitate before ordaining *any* man or woman who is promiscuous or adulterous. To do otherwise is to place a potential seducer in the ministry. But what of men and women who are in committed, monogamous sex unions? Should the church treat them as they would a man or woman in a traditional marriage? In my view, the church would be wise not to withhold a blessing if the partners are motivated by mutual love and if their union promises to be permanent. But the church need not pretend that gay unions meet the traditional definition of marriage.

Inclusiveness in any case rests on forgiveness. As C. S. Lewis once noted, "Everyone says forgiveness is a lovely idea until they have something to forgive."[8] An unforgiving faith may be a mile wide but it will always be less than an inch deep.

9. Learn the faith.

Faith is substance as well as practice. To protest that "I believe" is meaningless unless one can specify the content of one's faith.

Nor can one escape articulating one's beliefs by simply affirming that "I believe in God" and leaving it at that. That is an expression of trust, not of faith. "I believe, Lord; help my unbelief" is the prayer of a saint who both trusts God and admits his temptation to doubt. All believers find themselves in that position.

But it does not excuse them from affirming the *content* of God's revelation. It took Christendom four centuries to forge the profession of faith we have come to call the Nicene Creed. That creed is not a prayer, nor is it especially inspiring. It is not religion itself. Rather, it is like the table of contents on a package of food. It tells us what is in there to nourish us. A shorter statement of this content is known as The Apostles' Creed:

> I believe in God, the Father almighty,
>   creator of heaven and earth.
> I believe in Jesus Christ, his only Son, our Lord.
>   He was conceived by the power of the Holy Spirit
>   and born of the Virgin Mary.
> He suffered under Pontius Pilate,
>   was crucified, died, and was buried.
> He descended to the dead.
> On the third day he rose again.
> He ascended into heaven,
>   and is seated at the right hand of the Father.
> He will come again to judge the living and the dead.
> I believe in the Holy Spirit,
>   the holy catholic church,
>   the communion of saints,
>   the forgiveness of sins,
>   the resurrection of the body,
>   and the life everlasting.[9]

Admittedly, creeds are only composed of words, and can be misinterpreted. But God spoke, and Jesus spoke, so we are wise not to ignore what they took the trouble to reveal in human words.

Scripture is a verbal account of revelation—of God acting and speaking. Admittedly, one can become so devoted to the Bible that it approaches idolatry—substituting a book for the living God. Still, to encounter the Scriptures is to know what God has said to all of us that applies to us equally. To seek special revelation upon which to build a private faith is to make God one's personal possession and to denigrate the community of believers that is the church. To construct one's faith on private revelation alone is to ensure that it will never be more than an inch deep.

10. Practice the faith publicly.

Peter Maurin, cofounder (with Dorothy Day) of the Catholic Worker movement, insisted that the test of faith rests in action. For humanity's sake, he argued, the church must speak loudly to government and business alike. By the church he meant every Christian.

"When religion has nothing to do with politics," he said, "politics is only factionalism: 'Let's turn the rascals out so our good friends can get in!' When religion has nothing to do with business, business is only commercialism: 'Let's get what we can while the getting's good!'"

At the same time it sought justice and jobs for ordinary Americans, the movement insisted that individual Christians retain personal responsibilities they cannot cede to government and institutions. Maurin was impressed that the earliest believers were admired by pagans for their personal generosity with one another: "See how they love one another!" bystanders marveled.

To be sure, piety easily becomes pretentious. Jesus himself decried the religious show-offs: "Believe me, they have had all the reward they are going to get" (Matthew 6:2).

It is ironic that, despite America's mile-wide faith, religion remains a taboo topic for polite conversation in society, as if we were ashamed of God. Meanwhile, hypocrisy abounds in public life. Politicians routinely pronounce their piety but casually vote against their beliefs, protesting that faith is a private affair and that they were elected to reflect the wishes of the voters.

The churches do not help matters when they disagree with one another about the Gospel's demands on public policy. But honest disagreement should not deter the churches and individual believers from speaking out and acting out. If the church were meant to be exclusively other-worldly, then it was pointless for God to walk the earth and give rules for living this side of eternity.

Years ago, when I was first moved to produce a book, I addressed it to people like myself—reluctant Christians. That book was titled *Growing in Faith*. My hope was that I could help myself and others to overcome the reluctance to act out our beliefs publicly:

> I suggest that our reluctance to respond to Jesus stems not from any disagreement with him but from a fear of going out on a limb, of trying and falling flat. We hate the prospect of appearing foolish. If we're going to try to act like Christians, we don't want to appear amateurish about it, but that appears to be the best we can expect from ourselves since Jesus's standards are Olympian![10]

The church itself must risk appearing foolish when it confronts a permissive, self-indulgent culture with a faith that insists on simplicity, humility, truth-telling, peace-making, and forgiving, and expects persecution for its efforts. So be it. Any Great Awakening must lead to action.

Early in the new millennium I challenged an audience of Quakers at North Carolina's Guilford College, asking them, "Why did Quakers stop quaking?" A man in his eighties gave this testimony:

> I know why I don't quake. I don't ask God the hard questions about what he requires me to do with my life. I'm afraid that if I ask him God will tell me something difficult that I'm unwilling to do. But if I was willing to listen to him, and do what he demands, then I'd start quaking.[11]

Whether he realizes it, that man holds the key to the next Great Awakening of religious faith in America.

O God of earth and altar,
Bow down and hear our cry.
Our earthly rulers falter,
 Our people drift and die;
 The walls of gold entomb us,
The swords of scorn divide;
Take not thy thunder from us,
 But take away our pride.

From all that terror teaches,
From lies of tongue and pen,
From all the easy speeches
That comfort cruel men,
From sale and profanation
Of honor and the sword,
From sleep and from damnation
Deliver us good Lord.

Tie in a living tether
The prince and priest and thrall,
Bind all our lives together,
Smite us and save us all.
In ire and exultation,
Aflame with faith, and free,
Lift up a living nation,
A single sword to thee.
   —G. K. Chesterton (1874-1938)

Author's
Notes
and
Acknowledgments

THE SUBJECT OF *THE FUTURE OF CHRISTIAN FAITH IN America* was suggested by a series of lectures I was invited to deliver at the venerable Chautauqua Institution on the future of faith in America. Chautauqua, in northwestern New York State near Lake Erie, was founded in 1874 as a summer school for Sunday school teachers. It has evolved into a year-round utopian community of 7,500 residents devoted to the highest ideals of spirit and intellect. More than 142,000 people visit Chautauqua each year to enjoy its summer programs. Its resident historian, Ross Mackenzie, remarks: "There is an unarticulated awareness of the sacred and the holy in the whole community because of the natural surroundings and because of the created human beauty. Civil discourse, friendship, dance, music, all of these . . . give us an awareness of the holy."

At Chautauqua my wife and I were the grateful guests of Joan Brown Campbell, longtime head of the National Council of Churches and now director of religion at Chautauqua. Journalists depend on reliable sources. The distinguished editorialist David Bowes introduced me to Chautauqua and encouraged me to speak there. I dedicate this book to our friendship.

I am especially grateful to my editors, Michelle L. N. Cook and Michael Wilt, for their patience and professionalism, and to Ann Rezny for her cover design.

In this undertaking, as in all, my wife, Rebecca, was my most reliable source and loving critic.

Sources

Chapter 1

1. Quoted by William F. Buckley Jr. "Let Us Pray?" *National Review,* October 10, 1994.
2. Will Herberg, *Protestant, Catholic, Jew* (Garden City, N. Y.: Doubleday Anchor, 1960), 260.
3. Robert D. Putnam, "Religious Participation," in *Bowling Alone* (New York: Simon & Schuster, 2000).
4. Herberg, 2.
5. Ibid., 258.
6. Ibid., 263.
7. Putnam, 72.
8. Ibid., 67.
9. Martin Marty, *The New Shape of American Religion* (New York: Harper, 1959), 13.
10. Putnam, 71.
11. Wade Clark Roof and William McKinney, *American Mainline Religion* (Piscataway, N.J.: Rutgers University Press, 1987), 16-17.
12. Ibid., 18-19.
13. Putnam, 75.
14. Ibid., 76.
15. *The Washington Post,* Sept. 18, 2001, A3.
16. Thomas C. Reeves, *The Empty Church* (New York: Free Press, 1996), 6-9.
17. Putnam, 123.
18. Herberg, 3.
19. Ibid., 123.
20. Ibid., 124.
21. Reeves, 67.
22. Daniel J. Boorstin, *The Americans*, vol. 1 (New York: Random House, 1958), 8.
23. *Encyclopedia Britannica,* 15th edition, 1988, vol. 6, 870.
24. Boorstin, 4.
25. Jeremy Paxman, *The English: A Portrait of a People* (New York: Penguin, 1999), 3-4.
26. Gallup Poll, 1988, cited in Reeves; Roper-Newsweek Poll, June 2, 1998.

Chapter 2

1. Alexis de Tocqueville, *Democracy in America* (New York: New American Library, 1958), 189.
2. Quoted by Michael Novak of the American Enterprise Institute at the Library of Congress in 1999.
3. de Tocqueville, 187.
4. Ibid., 189.
5. Roy P. Basker (ed.), *The Collected Works of Abraham Lincoln* (New Brunswick, N.J., 1953), VI, 155-156.
6. Thomas C. Reeves, *The Empty Church* (New York: Free Press, 1996), 38.
7. *National Review*, 87.

8. *The Washington Post,* December 8, 1999, A7.
9. Ibid.
10. George Barna, *The Barna Report: What Americans Believe: An Annual Survey of Values and Religious Views in the United States* (Ventura, Calif.: Regal Books, 1996), 11.
11. Phyllis A. Tickle, *God-Talk in America* (New York: Crossroad, 1997), 10.
12. *Christianity Today,* March 25, 2000, 15.
13. *The Washington Post,* November 18, 1999, B1.
14. Alan Wolfe, "Quiet Faith," in *One Nation, After All* (New York: Penguin, 1999), 39-87.
15. Charles Trueheart, "The Next Church," *The Atlantic Monthly,* Nov. 1999 (cover story).
16. Ibid., 20.
17. Ibid.
18. Ibid.
19. Ibid.
20. Ibid., 21.
21. Ibid., 22.
22. Ibid.

Chapter 3
1. Norman Vincent Peale, *In God We Trust* (New York: Thomas Nelson, 1994).
2. Ibid., 38.
3. Ibid., 39.
4. Ibid.
5. Newsweek-Roper poll, *Newsweek,* June 3, 1998.
6. Rosabeth Moss Kanter, *Commitment and Community* (Cambridge, Mass.: Harvard University Press, 1972), 39.
7. I give an account of the major American faith-based utopian movements in a forthcoming book, *Heaven on Earth.*
8. Alan Wolfe, "Quiet Faith," in *One Nation, After All* (New York: Penguin, 1999), 55.
9. Peale, 42.
10. See Robert H. Schuller, *Life's Not Fair, But God Is Good.* (New York: Thomas Nelson, 1994).
11. See Fulton J. Sheen, *Peace of Soul* (New York: McGraw-Hill, 1949).
12. See Harold S. Kushner, *When Bad Things Happen to Good People* (New York: Schocken Books, 1989), 5.
13. Ibid.
14. Charles Trueheart, "The Next Church," *The Atlantic Monthly,* Nov. 1999 (cover story), 89.
15. George M. Marsden, *Fundamentalism and American Culture* (Oxford: Oxford University Press, 1980), 158.
16. See William James, *The Varieties of Religious Experience* (New York: New American Library, 1958), 69.
17. Marilyn Ferguson, *The Aquarian Conspiracy: Personal and Social Transformation in the 1980s* (Los Angeles: J. P. Tarcher, 1981), 49.
18. Alexis de Tocqueville, quoted by Ferguson.
19. Ferguson, 19.
20. Ibid.
21. Harvey Cox, *Fire from Heaven* (Reading, Mass.: Addison-Wesley, 1995), 181.
22. See Jeffrey Gros, Eamon McManus, and Ann Riggs, *Introduction to Ecumenism* (Mahwah, N. J.: Paulist Press, 1998).
23. "Denominations Reach Accord," *The Washington Post,* October 28, 1999, A3.
24. Ibid.
25. Cox, 12.
26. Ibid., 191.
27. Marsden, 159.

Chapter 4

1. Written by Bryan Appleyard.
2. C. S. Lewis, *The Four Loves* (New York: Harcourt Brace, 1960), 140.
3. Alan Wolfe, "Quiet Faith," in *One Nation, After All* (New York: Penguin, 1999), 55.
4. Kenneth L. Woodward, "Dead End for the Mainline?" *Newsweek*, Aug. 9, 1993.
5. See C. Kirk Hadaway, Penny Cong Marler, and Mark Chaves, "What the Polls Don't Show: A Closer Look at Church Attendance," *American Sociological Review* (December 1993), 751
6. Wade Clark Roof and William McKinney, *American Mainline Religion* (Piscataway, N.J.: Rutgers University Press, 1987), 56.
7. Hadaway, 741-752.
8. Ibid., 745.
9. Harold Bloom, *The American Religion: The Emergence of the Post-Christian Nation* (New York: Simon & Schuster, 1992), 13.
10. Ibid., 72.
11. Ralph Waldo Emerson, "Self-Reliance." He added: "I like the silent church before the service begins, better than any preaching."
12. Crane Brinton, *The Shaping of the Modern Mind* (New York: Mentor Books, 1959), 113.
13. Thomas C. Reeves, *The Empty Church* (New York: Free Press, 1996), 69-102.
14. Ibid., 70.
15. C. S. Lewis, *God in the Dock: Essays on Theology and Ethics* (Grand Rapids, Mich.: Eerdmans, 1970), 58.
16. David Yount, *Be Strong and Courageous: Letters to My Children about Being Christian* (Lanham, Md.: Sheed & Ward, 2000).
17. William Murchison, *Reclaiming Morality in America* (New York: Thomas Nelson, 1994), 122.
18. Woodward, 46.
19. Ibid.
20. Reeves, 153.
21. Ibid., 3.
22. Ibid., 47.
23. Reeves, 10-13.
24. Ibid, 16.
25. Ibid, 16.
26. Reeves, 18.
27. Ibid.
28. Ibid.
29. Ibid.
30. Reeves, 18-19.
31. *Milwaukee Journal*, July 3, 1993.
32. *The Wall Street Journal*, July 19, 1994.

Chapter 5

1. Stephen L. Carter, *The Culture of Disbelief* (New York: Basic Books, 1993), 44-45.
2. Robert D. Putnam, "Religious Participation," in *Bowling Alone* (New York: Simon & Schuster, 2000), 78.
3. See Janet Forsythe Fishburn, *The Fatherhood of God and the Victorian Family: The Social Gospel in America* (Philadelphia: Fortress, 1981).
4. See David Yount, *What Are We to Do? Living the Sermon on the Mount* (Lanham, Md.: Sheed & Ward, 2002), x.
5. Tom W. Smith, "The Emerging Twenty-First Century American Family," General Social Survey Social Change Report no. 42, National Opinion Research Center, University of Chicago, November 24, 1999, 2-5.
6. Ibid.
7. Ibid.
8. *The Washington Post*, January 10, 2001, A4.
9. Charles W. Colson and Ellen Santilli Vaughn, *Against the Night: Living in the New Dark Ages* (Ventura, Calif.: Servant Publications, 1999), 194.

10. *The Washington Post,* March 3, 2000, A27.
11. Ibid., A5.
12. Ibid.
13. Frederick M. Gedicks, "The Religious, the Secular, and the Antithetical," *Capital University Law Review 20* (1991), 113.
14. Robert Wuthnow, *The Restructuring of American Religion* (Princeton, N. J.: Princeton University Press, 1988), 244.
15. Carter, 51-52.
16. Fred Kaplon, *Gore Vidal: A Biography* (New York: Doubleday, 1999), 750ff.
17. "Outlook," *The Washington Post,* December 5, 1999, 1.
18. Ibid., 2.

Chapter 6
1. John Bartlett, *Familiar Quotations,* 15th edition (New York: Little, Brown, 1980), 909.
2. *Forbes,* January 22, 2000, 26.
3. Ibid.
4. William Blake, "Jerusalem," *The Complete Poems,* Alicia Ostriker, ed. (New York: Penguin, 1977), 635.
5. Ibid.
6. See Janet Forsythe Fishburn, *The Fatherhood of God and the Victorian Family: The Social Gospel in America* (Philadelphia: Fortress, 1981).
7. *The Washington Post,* February 18, 2000, A5.
8. John W. Wright, ed., *The New York Times Almanac* (New York: Penguin, 2002), 321-24.
9. *The Washington Post,* March 31, 2000, A26.
10. See Thomas C. Reeves, *The Empty Church* (New York: Free Press, 1996).
11. Ibid., 6-7.
12. Ibid., 8.
13. Ibid.
14. Ibid.
15. Ibid.
16. Ibid., 9.
17. Ibid., 6-7.
18. *National Review,* October 10, 1994.
19. Paul Johnson, "Hope for the Millennium," *Reader's Digest,* December, 1999 (cover story).

Chapter 7
1. *The Washington Post,* September 15, 2001, 1.
2. *The Sunday Times* (London), November 25, 2001.
3. John Bartlett, *Familiar Quotations,* 15th edition (New York: Little, Brown, 1980), 522.
4. Ibid.
5. *The Sunday Times* (London), November 25, 2001.
6. Ibid.
7. *Los Angeles Times,* September 20, 2001, A17.
8. *National Geographic* news release, September 18, 2001.
9. Ibid.
10. Ibid.
11. See Alan Wolfe, *Moral Freedom: The Search for Virtues in a World of Choice* (New York: W. W. Norton and Co., 2001).
12. Wolfe, *One Nation After All* (New York: Penguin, 1999), ch. 2.
13. Robert D. Putnam, "Religious Participation," in *Bowling Alone* (New York: Simon & Schuster, 2000), ch. 4.
14. Alexis de Tocqueville, *Democracy in America* (New York: New American Library, 1958), 89.
15. Putnam, 67.
16. C. Eric Lincoln, "The Black Church and Black Self-Determination" (paper

presented at the annual meeting of the Association of Black Foundation Executives, Kansas City, Missouri, April 1989).
17. Putnam, 72-73.
18. Ibid., 74.
19. See David Yount, "Why Did Quakers Stop Quaking?" *Quaker Life*, March 2002, 12-13.
20. Putnam, 76.
21. Ibid., 78.
22. Ibid.
23. Wolfe, *One Nation, After All*, ch. 2.
24. Ibid., 82.
25. See Thomas C. Reeves, *The Empty Church* (New York: Free Press, 1996), ch. 6.
26. Harold Bloom, *The American Religion: The Emergence of the Post-Christian Nation* (New York: Simon & Schuster, 1992), ch. 1.

Chapter 8
1. Johnson, Hoge, and Luidens, "Mainline Churches: The Real Reason for Decline," *First Things*, March, 1993, 14.
2. Thomas C. Reeves, *The Empty Church* (New York: Free Press, 1996), 169.
3. Wade Clark Roof, *A Generation of Seekers* (San Francisco: HarperSanFrancisco, 1986). 185-186.
4. Reeves, 170-171.
5. Ibid., 171.
6. Ibid., 173.
7. George Gallup Jr. and Jim Castelli, *The People's Religion: American Faith in the 90s* (New York: MacMillan Publishing Co., 1989), 253.
8. Reeves, 186.
9. Ibid., 187.
10. Ibid., 181.
11. Ibid.
12. Ibid., 187.
13. Ibid., 189.
14. *The Wall Street Journal*, July 14, 1995.
15. Reeves, 198.
16. Ibid., 199-200.
17. C. S. Lewis, *Mere Christianity* (New York: Macmillan Publishing Co., 1960), 15.
18. Gallup Poll News Service, January 9, 2003.
19. Gallup Poll News Service, December 18, 2002.
20. Gallup Poll News Service, January 9, 2003.
21. Ibid.
22. Ibid.
23. George Gallup Jr. and D. Michael Lindsay, *The Gallup Guide: Reality Check for 21st Century Churches* (Loveland, Colo.: Group Publishing, 2002), 11.
24. Gallup Poll News Service, January 9, 2003.
25. Gallup and Lindsay, 8.
26. Gallup Poll News Service, January 9, 2003.
27. Gallup and Lindsay, 9.
28. Ibid.
29. Ibid., 17-18.
30. Sally Stuart, "Write Markets," *The Christian Communicator*, February 2003, 11.
31. Johnson, Hoge, and Luidens, 203.
32. Ibid., 204.
33. Ibid., 204-205.
34. Ibid., 205.
35. Ibid., 208.
36. Loren B. Mead, *Five Challenges for the Once and Future Church* (Bethesda, Md.: Alban Institute, 1996), vii.
37. Ibid., 1.
38. Ibid., 5.

39. Ibid., 6.
40. Ibid., 15.
41. Ibid. 18.
42. Ibid., 26.
43. Ibid., 26-27.
44. Ibid., 27-28.
45. Ibid., 30.
46. Ibid., 34.
47. Ibid., 42.
48. Ibid., 50.
49. Ibid., 52.
50. Ibid.
51. Ibid., 55.
52. Ibid., 63.
53. Ibid.
54. Ibid., 80.
55. Ibid., 85-86.
56. Interview in The *Sunday Times* (London, 2000).
57. Loren B. Mead, *More Than Numbers: The Way Churches Grow* (Bethesda, Md.: Alban Institute, 1993), 13.
58. Ibid., 51.
59. Ibid., 52.
60. Ibid., 54.
61. Ibid., 78-79.
62. Ibid., 98.
63. John Bartlett, *Familiar Quotations,* 15th edition (New York: Little, Brown, 1980), 742.

Chapter 9

1. Joseph Wood Krutch, "Love—or the Life and Death of a Value," in *The Modern Temper* (New York: Harvest Books, 1956), 58.
2. Norman Mailer, interviewed in The *Guardian*, September 7, 2002.
3. Krutch, 78.
4. Ibid.
5. Robert D. Putnam, "Religious Participation," in *Bowling Alone* (New York: Simon & Schuster, 2000), 72 ff.
6. Thomas C. Reeves, *The Empty Church* (New York: Free Press, 1996), 12-13.
7. Alan Wolfe, *Moral Freedom: The Search for Virtues in a World of Choice* (New York: W. W. Norton and Co., 2001), 23 ff.
8. John Bartlett, *Familiar Quotations,* 15th edition (New York: Little, Brown, 1980), 842.
9. English translation of The Apostle's Creed by the International Consultation on English Texts. Used by permission.
10. David Yount, *Growing in Faith: A Guide for the Reluctant Christian* (New York: Penguin, 1995), 4.
11. David Yount, "Why Did Quakers Stop Quaking?" *Quaker Life,* March 2002, 13.